THE POWER OF YES

VOLUME ONE IMPACT

by LINKEDIN AND TOWN HALL ACHIEVER OF THE YEAR
EY NOMINEE ENTREPRENEUR OF THE YEAR
GRAND HOMAGE LYS DIVERSITY

Dr BAK NGUYEN, DMD

TO ALL THOSE LOOKING FOR MORE,
FOR BETTER, FOR INNER PEACE AND GROWTH.
THE ANSWER IS WITHIN YOUR POWER.

by Dr BAK NGUYEN

ISBN: 978-1-989536-47-6

ABOUT THE AUTHOR

From Canada, **Dr BAK NGUYEN**, Nominee Ernst and Young Entrepreneur of the year, Grand Homage Lys DIVERSITY, and LinkedIn & TownHall Achiever of the year. Dr Bak is a cosmetic dentist, CEO and founder of Mdex & Co. His company is revolutionizing the dental field. Speaker and motivator, he wrote 72 books over 36 months accumulating many world records (to be officialized).

- **ENTREPRENEURSHIP**
- **LEADERSHIP**
- **QUEST OF IDENTITY**
- **DENTISTRY AND MEDICINE**
- **PARENTING**
- **CHILDREN BOOKS**
- **PHILOSOPHY**

In 2003, he founded Mdex, a dental company upon which in 2018, he launched the most ambitious private endeavour to reform the dental industry, Canada wide. Philosopher, he has close to his heart the quest of happiness of the people surrounding him, patients and colleagues alike. In 2020, he launched an International collaborative initiative named **THE ALPHAS** to share knowledge and for Entrepreneurs and Doctors to thrive through the Greatest Pandemic and Economic depression of our time.

In 2016, he co-found with Tranie Vo, Emotive World Incorporated, a tech research company to use technology to empower happiness and sharing. U.A.X. the ultimate audio experience is the landmark project on which the team is advancing, utilizing the technics of the movie industry and the advancement in ARTIFICIAL INTELLIGENCE to save the book industry and to upgrade the continuing education space.

These projects have allowed Dr Nguyen to attract interests from the international and diplomatic community and he is now the center of a global discussion in the wellbeing and the future of the health profession. It is in that matter that he shares his thoughts and encourages the health community to share their own stories.

"It's not worth it go through it alone! Together, we stand, alone, we fall."

Motivational speaker and serial entrepreneur, philosopher and author, from his own words, Dr Nguyen describes himself as a dentist by circumstances, an entrepreneur by nature and a communicator by passion.

He also holds recognitions from the Canadian Parliament and the Canadian Senate.

THE POWER OF YES

VOLUME ONE IMPACT

by Dr BAK NGUYEN

WRITING BOOKS ALLOWED ME TO EVOLVE AT THE SPEED OF MY THOUGHTS
-DR. BAK NGUYEN

INTRODUCTION

BY DR BAK NGUYEN

Keep your **pride** in check
And you'll be just fine.
It's not that hard,
We only need to choose.
We **choose**.

Even with only 10% access to our brains,
We are **ingenious**
And made it this far!

Because we were smart enough
To build on everyone's 10%.
That was the How.
The real greatness comes from
The What.

With a **nation of hearts**
Beating as **one**,
We will achieve greatness.
With our **Will** to make the day,
To make the **difference**,
To **matter**.

I am writing these words as I just finished writing my 72nd book within 36 months, with 8 days before the dateline. But I promised myself that after the 72nd book and the new world record, I would spend some time editing and cleaning my record.

This is it. Some of the books that my co-authors never delivered, I will have to fill-in for their parts. The original idea of this book, **YES BY DEFAULT**, was originally comprised of my first 36 titles after 18 months of writing. Well, editing and packaging, it made more sense to me to respect the number of the Dragon: 8 chapters per book.

8 chapters will comprise the writing of my journey of 12 months as an author, writing 223 922 words in 2 languages. When you write as much, you start to lose the count. Each book is unique and an experience by itself, but once it is over, you move on to your next adventure just as it should be in life. Writing books was among the best things I decided to try.

> **"WRITING BOOKS ALLOWED ME TO EVOLVE AT THE SPEED OF MY THOUGHTS."**
> DR BAK NGUYEN

Once the thoughts are clear, they begin to shape my actions and decisions, slowly shaping literally the world around me. It all started when I accepted to speak on stage for an entrepreneurial conference where I was supposed to appear after Michelle Obama! That was 18 months ago and it never happened. I was ready though.

Michelle Obama scared the crap out of me and I got prepared by writing **TED talk**, 21 of them to be precise. A **TED**

talk is mainly a self-contained chapter in which I share what I learned and how I learned it from my experiences. I wrote as I speak and I wrote in English since I was projecting myself speaking on stage. 21 chapters later, I added an introduction and a conclusion and voilà! Here was my first book on business.

Two weeks later, my first book, **SYMPHONY OF SKILLS** was completed. It all started because I said **YES** to a producer and friend of mine, Thierry Lindor. Looking back, it was such a crazy and unexpected ride. Two write a book within 14 days was a discovery, maybe the setting of a new world record. That, I still have to verify.

The world records came to appear on the table as I was forced to write my second book, the french version of the first one. 25k words in English became 35k words in French, 2 weeks and 6 hours later. Well, it is there that I learned that no one ever written and published, at least in Quebec, in 2 different languages, left alone, writing them within a month! That was 2 world's firsts or 2 world records right from the start.

And yes, my world records still have to be officialized, I am just too busy writing and changing the numbers to stop for inspection. I've done it. There are there for people to see, read and enjoy. My job is not to prove or to sell, my job is to share and to keep sharing. That, I learned on the way, writing.

Well, writing, believe it or not, is not one of my strong suits. I do not like to read, at least written books. For the last 15 years, most of the books I read are in audio format. Those, I love. I started writing from my iPhone to prepare for the stage. I woke up 1, then 2 hours earlier in the morning to write. Each morning, I woke up by myself, without any alarm.

Writing **SYMPHONY OF SKILLS** (book #1) was a charm after I started opening up about my past failures. Writing the French version, **LA SYNERGIE DES SENS** (book #2), was a burden, since I had the impression to work for a second time on the same book.

Trust me, that wasn't the same book, not at all. Writing from English to French, I did more than translating my own words, I kept writing, kept pushing. In a way, the French version is, in fact, version 1.5 of **SYMPHONY OF SKILLS**. On that one, the second book, I took a beating. But the mark of writing both of them within a month kept me going. Those 2 are 21 chapters each!!!

And then, I took a break, celebrating my new accomplishments. But I kept waking up at 5 in the morning without any alarm. I stood there looking at the sun for a few weeks and decided to jump right back in, writing **LEADERSHIP, PANDORA'S BOX** (book #3). A few weeks later, I was done, again! Then, I started **IDENTITY** (book #4).

I did not plan for any of these to happen. So why did I keep writing? I did so because I can, and because it became my "me time". You see, every time I write, it's not me writing but my sub-conscience. I feel like every morning, that's the time I allow myself to speak to my inner self. As words are coming out, I am as surprised and amazed as any of you, surprised by the line of thoughts and intimidated by the speed and the volume.

As you know, I usually write from my iPhone, using notes. Then, I paste it into my MacBook. Every time I open the files on my MAC, I got intimidated for a few minutes. Then, I recognized each of the words I just wrote and things go back to normal.

It took me up to **LEADERSHIP** (book #3) to understand that I was in it by myself. Artists I hired for my books' covers were not working out, making me lose much time back and forth as the artistic results was so-so. I needed help with editing and publishing too. These too did not turn the way I would have wished. After 3 months waiting, the biggest publishers of Quebec said thank you but no thank you.

17

Rejection is hard, but to take 3 months for it was not acceptable. Please keep in mine that speed is my power. Actually, speed is my nature. And I was meeting with the high executives of these publishing companies referred to me by my friends and business partners. Speed was not part of the DNA of that industry.

I even had the impression that they did not like mine. Nonetheless, I was too busy to be hurt, I kept writing, seeing patients and leading my company and my industry into the new era of dentistry. On that, we just receive millions as new investments into the new expansion of **Mdex**.

Me embracing the stage was primarily a business public relation exercise. Little did I knew how far it would lead me. 6 months after I started writing, I finally gave my first speaking event at the John Molson School of Business, Concordia University.

Thierry organized that one. I was ready, I did my job, I was within my comfort zone since Michelle Obama wasn't scheduled to appear on stage. Instead, the anchor was Casey Neistat, the super YOU TUBER star.

Until that day, I never heard of the man. To be honest, if I had a chance to escape, I would have, but I met with Thierry at the door of the conference room when he invited me to join the main event of the day. "Of course!" I said out of friendship. I went in and for the first half of Casey's talk, I couldn't find any way to connect.

Usually, when you meet with someone, there are only two things that can happen. Either you connect and the energy goes up or you compare and the energy goes down. I knew that. But I tried for half an hour and I couldn't find any way to connect. So I started comparing.

"MY LIFE CHANGED BEFORE THE END OF HIS SPEECH."

For years, I was better off then Casey as we were both failures in our dreams to become movie directors. But then, YOU TUBE came around and Casey started rising. Not because of YOU TUBE but because he never stopped.

He and I are both geniuses in creation, we can paint emotions with our minds, the difference was that he painted his, put them online and went on to his next painting. He did that again and again as he got better time after time.

That was my mistake, as a doctor, I am shaped pretty square and I have to plan for homeruns before I create. Once I created, I stood in line waiting for the right opportunity to launch, hiring and listening to experts from the last century… Standing in line, that's the best way to stall your momentum.

19

As he was generous about his creativity and embraced life and its opportunity, I was playing it safe, being cheap with my own creativity and not letting it space to grow. No more, thank you Casey, you changed my life, you showed me where I went wrong.

Since that day, I start saying **YES** to almost everything to **reset my mind** and to **expand my openness**. It was a bet and a crazy idea, but I felt its calling. I wrote it down and started saying **YES**.

"YES, I AM A MAN OF MY WORD. YES!"

DR BAK NGUYEN

From there, I met with all kind of people. Saying **YES** brought me to be the co-anchor of a speaking event at the Olympic Stadium a month and a half later. I went on to receive the **nomination for Ernst and Young for entrepreneur of the year**. That nomination pushed me to published within a month my 7th book, **CHANGING THE WORLD FROM A DENTAL CHAIR**. From there, things just got faster and crazier.

I won't say that all the people I met were good and smart people. Often my preconceived ideas were all true, but since I was obliged to stay open, it gave me the chance to realize that those preconceived ideas were only about 10 to 15% of the person, not the whole. Some stayed for a little while and left, some became good friends, brothers, some even mentors.

I was still celebrating and writing new world records. By then, By then, every new book I wrote was a new world record. And then, boom! I learned about my first public defeat: I did not make the cut for the next phase of the **Ernst and Young Entrepreneur of the year award**. That nomination fueled my drive for the last few months after the John Molson School of business and the Olympic Stadium.

To cope, I realized that I had about a month and a half before my first-anniversary writing. And I had 7 books to show. What if I could make it a round number. What about setting the next world record of 12 books written over 12 months? This would surely fade away the shame of defeat!

Well, this book is that story. The story of my first-year writing. **THE POWER OF YES** volume One is the story of that crazy journey, the journey of a man discovering his powers as he spoke. Well, to be more accurate, as he wrote and walked his own words.

To be honest, this book was supposed to be a cheat. I always knew that by the end of my 12 months saying YES, I would compile all of my INTRODUCTIONS, which served as my journal's entries since I started writing.

That night, I had nothing to do and I started compiling the introductions one after the next. Just for the fun of it, I didn't start from the time of Casey's conference, but I started from the beginning of my journey as an author.

It was supposed to be a simple exercise, pasting texts into my new book, each of my INTRODUCTIONS since day one. It took most of the night, copying and re-editing every single one of them. Then, I had to structure the table of content to realize that I was better writing new books than to read and edit my old ones. But it was too late to back out from this one.

"KEEP YOUR MIND OPEN AND YOUR HEART LIGHT, TO EMBRACE THE POSSIBILITIES."

DR BAK NGUYEN

By the next morning, I was up, a little hungover by last night lack of sleep but up and running as always. Then I realized that the intros alone would not be enough to tell you the story of my journey. I had to add it my conclusion and to make them work somehow.

But once we know what we want and stop complaining about the price, well, the potential in power is limitless. You still do not believe me? This story is not inspired by real-life events, this story is my life. Except for the introduction and the conclusion written much after the facts, you are reading the adventures and the challenges as they happened, and with the sight I had as they happened. You are literally walking in my shoes and seeing life through my eyes.

More than entertaining you, this book will show you the way to **ABUNDANCE** with the **POWER OF YES**, the power of seizing the day and to make the most out of it. With that, I had to develop tools and armors to leverage on. You will see the creation of those mindsets, where there are coming from and why they came to exist. Those mindsets and leverages, you will often find as quotes in my books.

This is my story, this is my journey. Even if things changed, went sideways and hurt, I kept my focus and I went through. I kept pushing and I became someone else.

Someone **better**,
Someone **stronger**,
Someone **hungrier**,
I became **more**.

"LIFE IS REALLY ABOUT THE CHOICES YOU ARE MAKING."

DR BAK NGUYEN

If you still doubt that you cannot change things or that the tide is too strong against you, well, think again. I am here to prove to you that it's never too late and it's not impossible. I started writing books and scoring **world records** on top of my daily occupation as a cosmetic dentist and a CEO.

The CEO job alone is twice the among of workload since I am aiming to change an entire industry. By the time I started writing, we were just about to open our first pilot project in downtown Montreal. **Mdex** occupies two floors in a prime commercial building in the heart of the Golden Square Mile, in Montreal, in the same neighborhood of the Ritz Carlton and the Museum of Fine Arts.

Needless to tell you of the burden of the financial stress I was putting on my shoulders. That bet could make me or break me!

There is also the dentist function, even only with three days a week, it takes much energy and concentration to deliver to each of my patient, one after the other. So as you see, my schedule was pretty tight already. The odds were for me to be buried under one of those two jobs.

"I OPENED MY SPIRIT AND I EMBRACED MY CALLING, NOT LETTING ANYTHING BEHIND."
DR BAK NGUYEN

12 months later, I am still a dentist in demand and loved by my patients. I am leading **Mdex & Co** and my Industry into a new era of sharing and collaboration and I am accumulating awards and recognitions for my mission, embracing Life!

Believe in yourself and embrace the possibilities of life. Life is greater than each of us. If you let it guide you, you'll be walking your destiny.

This is mine, may it inspires you to yours. This is the **POWER OF YES**, volume one. Welcome to the **Alphas**.

SOMEONE BETTER,
SOMEONE STRONGER,
SOMEONE HUNGRIER,
I BECAME MORE.
DR BAK NGUYEN.

EASE YOUR MIND AND FREE YOUR HEART, ➡ THIS IS ⬅ THE WAY TO HAPPINESS! -DR. BAK NGUYEN

CHAPTER 1

SYMPHONY OF SKILLS

SEPTEMBER 2017

BY DR BAK NGUYEN

"ARROGANCE IS NOT THE BRAGGING OF OUR KNOWLEDGE
BUT RATHER THE DENIAL OF OUR IGNORANCE."

DR BAK NGUYEN

We owe it to ourselves,
To know who, and what we are,
To understand the power of our mind
And elevate the spirit of the world with it.

Hope is only the beginning,
We are only the **beginning**.
The things we started,
The idea we pursued,
The stories of our adventures,
All of it will keep the **children** inspired
And ignite the **sacred fire** in their eyes,

No matter your age,
No matter your skin color,
We will find each other at some top
To share our stories.

We will only care for the differences we can **change**,
We will **inspire** more than we convince,
We will ride the day with our **heart** more than our head,
We will **love**, We will **do**, We will **share**.

As I took over the endeavour to write a book about entrepreneurship, I was scratching my head to know where to start. What about entrepreneurship? It is not like I went to school to become one. What new could I bring to the table? Of course, the idea of talking about what I did right was flattering, but I could write two, maybe three chapters at most on the matter, but a book? And it will be bragging as some people always twist things.

Then a very successful friend of mine, an awarded movie producer and director reminded me that it's okay to talk about our success, but it's more interesting and captivating to talk about our failures. About what I've learned from my mistakes and how I got back on track.

"THAT'S WHERE THE MEAT IS!"

That changes my whole perspective about this endeavour. If I can talk about my failures, the words were filling the pages by themselves, and pretty quickly. And they did, I am on my 9th chapter within 4 days!

Don't worry, I won't waste your time! There's a point to this process. As I started drafting the spine of my first book, the numbers of chapters and the subjects that I'll be covering. I had to make sense of the multiple stories I had in mind to entertain you about entrepreneurship.

It's then, that **ACROSS THE STAR**, a theme from Star Wars, by John Williams caught my attention. It was playing as I was driving my convertible and my head between the road, the sky, and the daydreams, it just hits me! Like that!

Thank you John Williams for the inspiration! I divided the book into small chapters, all independent from each other, in which I will be covering how entrepreneurship has been express through me or sometimes, how I wish it would have... Each chapter will have a quote as title, a quote that, by itself could inspire and summarize the whole chapter.

Sorry, I'm a lazy guy, I like it when it's short and easy. Each chapter is self-contained and can be read within 15 minutes. I want you to just pick it up, have a bite and move on with your life until the next chapter. Usually, an artist has to give enough of himself to attract your attention but hold back enough to keep some mystery. I know the rule, but I won't follow it.

What you will read within those pages are what is going on in my mind, in my soul. You'll be reading about what I've learned and my thought process. Some times, I will even share with you the pain attached to it! And if there is another book after this one, is because I've learned new things since.

As a journey, I wish to all entrepreneurs and aspirant entrepreneurs to take what they need from this and gain the confidence and the comfort that it's okay, that you are not alone, that WE are not alone. So let's start right away.

Entrepreneurship is the symphony of skills. Wrong to begin with. As entrepreneurs, to master a skill is just the first tiny little baby step. If we are not to take no for an answer, we will need to master many different skills and master how to speed up the learning curve. Much more, we will also need to master the management of all those skills and how to combine them together. I told you, I won't be wasting your time!

So the correct quote here would be: "Entrepreneurship, a symphony of skill sets that have to assemble into states of mind. " But written like that, it just lost all appeal.

Skill sets are many different skills mastered and interacting together in synergy, making the whole much greater than the sum of all its parts. In turn, those skillsets will fuse into a state of mind. One very important thing here is to know an entrepreneur does not know, he or she feels. The states of mind are the collective feeling we had when our skill sets are in action. Sounded somehow complex, it's just a lot of simple steps fused together. But you are already starting to break it down, aren't you?

You can master a skill to shine, but if you want to shine as an entrepreneur, a great and successful entrepreneur, you will need to master the skillsets until it turns into states of mind.

As you'll surf from a state of mind to the next, you'll have the power to do pretty much everything you put your mind into. Remember, knowledge is power and with great powers come great responsibilities. A piece of advice from *a friendly neighbourhood hero.*

I can't wait to witness the difference that you will bring to this world. You are drivers, thinkers, leaders, doers, whatever you need to be to get it done! I hope that my reflections will inspire you and somehow ease your pain in the learning process.

"NOWADAYS, SUCCESS DOESN'T COME FROM SECRECY BUT RATHER FROM SUCCESSFULLY SHARING KNOWLEDGE."

DR BAK NGUYEN

The paths to entrepreneurship are like the ones to Rome, they are many and they all lead to success. None of them are easy, there are no shortcuts, only the path you've created yourself. The journey is often a lonely one but, if you stay open despite the wounds and scars, you will meet with allies, who would help you achieve greatness.

Not all entrepreneurs will succeed, the ones who stayed behind are the ones who have quit somewhere on the path. To us entrepreneurs, only death will relieve us from duty, from fun.

"EASE YOUR MIND AND FREE YOUR HEART,
THIS IS THE WAY TO HAPPINESS!"

DR BAK NGUYEN

As skills etched into each of our scars, they slowly merged and combined into states of mind where the pain bear no weight. As much people had laughed once, they now praise and ask for more. It's not about them, it's about us. We are gifted, we are light, we are instruments of GOD to do good, we keep pushing forward with an **open mind** and **open heart** because we will not stop growing.

As we embraced our powers, we will stay mindful and kind of our surroundings, we will **respect** our partners and allies, we will build more than we will destroy, and we will always improve on it. Know who you are and how people see you. Have compassion for those who bear the pain of change.

"ARROGANCE IS NOT, PRIDE IS A PRISON."

DR BAK NGUYEN

In the darkness, when all seem lost, alone, our Tales will be our beacon of light, Momentum will be our horse to freedom, we will give, we will love, we will feel and we will never stop.

As the world of tomorrow depends on us to lead the way to a better, kinder, abundant one. Those are neither rules nor vain promises. These are what will be. This is our time, this is us. Entrepreneurs, my brothers and sisters, our paths will cross again and next time, I'll be the one learning from you, from your stories, from your minds.

Believe in yourself and embrace the possibilities of life. Life is greater than each of us. If you let it guide you, you'll be walking your destiny.

This is mine, may it inspires you to yours. This is the **POWER OF YES**, volume one. Welcome to the **Alphas**.

SOMEONE BETTER,
SOMEONE STRONGER,
SOMEONE HUNGRIER,
I BECAME MORE.
DR BAK NGUYEN.

WE ARE ALL BORN LITTLE, BUT SOME WILL CHOOSE TO STAY SMALL. THAT'S NOT THE SAME!
-DR. BAK NGUYEN

CHAPTER 2

LEADERSHIP

OCTOBER 2017

BY DR BAK NGUYEN

From the path, true **Loyalty**
Will keep us company.
We are all in this together,
As a **whole**.

We don't need to fight among ourselves
For the **carrots** anymore.
We can choose to stand tall,
Together, as a whole,
Go for the **elephants**,
And reach for the **stars**.

Life is **abundant**
If we choose to look beyond the horizon
Instead of looking at our feet.

We don't need to be *carrots eaters* forever. We have the freedom to choose for ourselves. And no one will do it for us. Stay hesitant and you just choose to stand behind. Nobody has chosen in your place even if you thought otherwise. Open your heart and your mind to yourself, and to Life!

Our world will be stronger with each one of us embracing our own freedom and make something out of our *compounded wills*! Together, as a whole, we are *citizens of the world*!

It's been less than two weeks since the last chapter of **SYMPHONY OF SKILLS**. I thought that it would take me some time before I start writing again. I was wrong. It's now the end of October and the pool is definitely closed until next May, I have to do something with the *momentum* from **SYMPHONY OF SKILLS**. The 20 laps energy will have to go on, so what's next?

I really did enjoy writing and learning about you, life and myself. Most people felt in love with **SYMPHONY OF SKILLS**. Many were wondering when I would write again, but this time for all, not just entrepreneurs. Each time, I smiled, not knowing what to respond.

In the meantime, I got involved in helping a friend to run for mayor. I applied some of the **SYMPHONY OF SKILLS'** theories to politic and suddenly, everything became clear, very clear!

I got caught in the charm and dove into some of the famous political speeches of Presidents and influencers of our century. Speeches from President John F. Kennedy, President Barack Obama, Mohamed Ali, Admiral William McRaven and, of course, Steve Jobs.

That is power, **words that can lift the spirit** and the world with it! You cannot stay immune to the words of those great men. It makes sense, it sounds right, and yet, they are talking about things that aren't yet!

"LIFE AND CREATIVITY COME FROM THE INTERACTION
OF TWO STRONG OPPOSITES."

DR BAK NGUYEN

I strongly believe that my third book, **LEADERSHIP, PANDORA'S BOX** will benefit much from, not just my thoughts and creativity but from the life resulting from the clashes of our minds. I say the third book here since, to stay true to my value and gratitude, I had to write **SYMPHONY OF SKILLS** twice, in English and then, in French.

If I have done something twice, that's two different books, and in the process, I had earned my *"master degree"* translating since by now, I know pretty well now the nuances and differences between French and English. It is not about the wording, by the style and the rhetoric.

In English, I have managed to keep my wording as close as possible to my speaking skills. It was possible for me to have a certain rhythm to my text, also like a march. In French, we use so much more words to arrive at the same result. 25 thousand words in English became 35 thousand words in French.

To keep the feeling vivid in my text, I had to use metaphors to keep the interest and the pace. I will say this: if in English

I had written marches, in French, the closer I could get was to valse.

This book, **LEADERSHIP, PANDORA'S BOX**, the next instalments of **SYMPHONY OF SKILLS**, is about how we should apply the powers of entrepreneurship into our world, for the greater good. The original title was:

"SOCIAL ENTREPRENEURSHIP, PANDORA'S BOX."

But after the first chapter about *Hope* was written, it became clearer that I have evolved since **SYMPHONY OF SKILLS**. This is **LEADERSHIP**. I do not pretend that I know *Leadership*, but I will tell you that *Leadership* is something that I feel clearly now.

"WE DO NOT BELIEVE IN COMPROMISE NOR HALF-TRUTH."
DR BAK NGUYEN

We will make a stand and aren't scared of a fight. More than that, we inspired to grow through this journey, to exchange with respect and learn from each other. I say we since we are all in this together.

This endeavour will be more than a philosophical exercise, I will cover 21 different themes of leadership that could impact the *world of tomorrow*. Yes, I want this book to matter and to inspire every one of us, citizens of the world, to make a difference. Each of the chapters will comprise of a presidential speech to inspire the next leaders among us. To do good.

"THE TRAIN OF LIFE IS ALWAYS RUNNING."

DR BAK NGUYEN

Life is a race.
Life is a journey.
Life is what greets us every morning

As long as we are willing
To wake up
And embrace the day.

Will today brings joy and victory or bears challenges and deceptions? The choice is ours to make. Always, Life is fulfilling and beautiful if we see the opportunity and face the **light of Hope**, leaving the **shadow of doubt** behind us. It's pure physics, it works every single time. So what will your day bring to our world?

To keep advancing, to push through the journey, we need to know what we want. For that to happen, we need to know who we are, really are, deep down. It's only when we've embraced ourselves completely, as part of the whole, that we start our journey, our legend. The **Quest of Identity** was only the *entrance* to the *canvas of Life*. We need to rise in control to start writing our destiny.

> "DON'T SPEND TOO MUCH OF YOUR LIFE LOOKING FOR A NAME.
> INSTEAD, SPEND TIME FORGING YOUR NAME IN THE FIRE OF LIFE."
>
> DR BAK NGUYEN

We are all in this together, as a whole. Each of us counts as a part of the team. We can bear more on our shoulders or look at others pulling the weight, only we, decide our role in the universe.

For as long as we've carried more than our own weight, we've made a difference. And then, we will notice that it wasn't that hard. We will want to do more, to pull more and before we even noticed, we've changed, we've grown.

Life can be lonely. Our **Quest of Identity** surely was but the journey of Life is a much greater quest. It doesn't have to be lonely. Choose your values and embrace your destiny.

"IT IS ONLY AS A WHOLE THAT WE START
TO GROW INTO GREATNESS."

DR BAK NGUYEN

To keep marching in the right direction, we will need help. The *smell of Death* will do just that, being that *friend*. It will keep us on our toes and challenge us to dare, beyond our imagination. Our greatest win will come the day we'll look her in the eyes and there will be no regrets left for her to feed on! We will eventually feel the *kiss of death*, but not yet!

Until then, **Time** will keep us company to remind us that *Life* is happening now, moving forward, always. It's a law of nature. But there are ways to bend the rule, to bend time itself. The power lays within each of our heart. The **power of Generosity**. The **power of Love**! Like Death, Time is an ally, caring for as long as we face the light of hope and move forward!

"TO LOVE IS TO RESPECT ONE'S RIGHT TO FIND OUT MORE OF ONESELF.
TO CARE IS TO BE THERE WHEN ONE'S REQUIRE
AN OPENED HEART TO SHARE WITH."

DR BAK NGUYEN

A generous Heart
Will never go hungry or poor.
It will stay hungry,
But never out of resources.

Safe, is part of the past.
Nothing great will comes from the known.
Yesterday, it might have been great,
But today, it's the new average.

The smartest among us only use 10% of their brain,
Why make such a big deal of the mind?
The Power is in the Heart.
This is where the universe vibes.

"LIFE IS REALLY ABOUT THE CHOICES YOU ARE MAKING."

DR BAK NGUYEN

Our hearts are the only ones that can stir through the tides of **Greed** and **Fear** and keep us on track. It's simple, natural. Our heart just needs to beat, consistently, strong, at its own pace until it is ready to grow into a *momentum*.

"DON'T STAND IN THE WAY OF A LOYAL LIONHEART
BECAUSE THERE IS NO VICTORY POSSIBLE."

DR BAK NGUYEN

Stay **humble** and we will avoid the falls on the road. Remember that to grow, we need to feed, every day, new tastes, new colors, new shapes. We are what we eat. If we eat the same things again and again, we will stay the same, left behind by the *train of Life*.

So why do we need a doorman to our minds and hearts? *Pride* is just a doorman that needs to keep the doors opened at all time and welcome Life in. **Pride is a door holder**, not a *gatekeeper*! Don't waste more time and energy on it.

And the rewards are great, trust me! A mind growing is the key to abundance. Its creativity will ease our way, every single time. We only need to allow it to be and to trust in ourselves. An open heart grows and, even with the scars adding up, will become stronger at each beat. If we keep growing, we will grow into our destiny, the *legend of the lionheart*.

"WE WERE ALL BORN LITTLE,
BUT SOME WILL CHOOSE TO STAY SMALL.
THAT'S NOT THE SAME."

DR BAK NGUYEN

To matter, we have to serve. To serve not ourselves, but the others. The legend is not about the goal but the journey. That's about us, our journey. To march forward and matter, we need leaders, lionhearts who will show the way, open the march and inspire others to join the *march of Life* and eventually, lead it one day.

Some of us are meant to be **lions**, others are **eagles** and others are **trees**. The strength of the lions is in their heart. The power of the eagles is in their minds and vision. The force of the trees is the unity of the forest. The *whole* is taking its vitality from the powers of each kind, from every single one of our hearts.

Feed yourself every day with new things and right values. Our world is not black and white nor good or bad. We made sure of that, by adapting. We can honour the past and build upon it. We are all in this together! Citizens of the world, entrepreneurs, lionhearts, be smart, be strong, be generous, be flexible, be kind. Master your heart, that's true leadership! Are you ready for greatness?

Believe in yourself and embrace the possibilities of life. Life is greater than each of us. If you let it guide you, you'll be walking your destiny.

This is mine, may it inspires you to yours. This is the **POWER OF YES**, volume one. Welcome to the **Alphas**.

SOMEONE BETTER,
SOMEONE STRONGER,
SOMEONE HUNGRIER,
I BECAME MORE.
DR BAK NGUYEN.

ONE'S STORY CAN ONLY BEGIN THE DAY ONE'S QUEST OF IDENTITY IS OVER

-DR. BAK NGUYEN

CHAPTER 3

IDENTITY

DECEMBER 2017

BY DR BAK NGUYEN

Life is balanced.

Life is given but **not free**.

Life is kind,

Life has provided us such **beauties**

To chase, to each, our taste!

That your way to **abundance**

Since there is so much of life

To taste and to discover

We do not all seek the same thing.

Leave the **carrots** and the **template** behind

Go for the **Elephants**!

Before long, we will have become bigger

Than the Elephant itself.

The only way to get bigger was to **grow**.

And growth can only occur

Within an **opened heart**

And an opened **mind**.

Happiness is not a quest, it is what comes with the quest. Stay opened, and *Happiness* will be your companion. Every time you'll invite it in, it will be on time at the door greeting you in *C major*! The journey doesn't have to be harder than it already is. *Happiness* will ease your way to *success* and *abundance*, even show you some *shortcuts*!

Remember that we were all little once, open your heart and mind and you don't have to stay small! That's the fate of the **Chicken Heart**. To grow or to stay small! The answer is in the heart, not the head! We are all *small-minded* people anyway, remember? Since the smartest among us use only *10% of their brain*. Why make such a *big deal* out of it?

> "WE WERE ALL PROFOUNDLY AND TRULY HAPPY AT THE BEGINNING.
> WE TRUST IN OURSELVES, WE KNOW THE WAY HOME!"
>
> DR BAK NGUYEN

It has been months since the beginning of my journey as an author. Three months ago, I started my rebirth with **SYMPHONY OF SKILLS**. It was a discovery to all, especially to me. Within two weeks, the first tome about my past of 20 years plus, as an entrepreneur went on paper and ready to go. Twenty-one themes of entrepreneurship wrapped with my own personal experiences and emotions.

The reception was just mind-blowing. To stay true to my roots and gratitude, I rewrote the entire book in French to honour my country and the legacy I inherited as a French Canadian, a Quebecer. I am too lazy to do something twice…!?! I beat myself up to the bone. Two weeks and 6 hours later, it was done!

To be honest, it was pretty challenging to stay motivated... but now, it's done! I had my story: I wrote two books in two different languages within a month!

Now I could rest or so I thought. As my team was connecting with the publishers and the other parties interested in the endeavour, I was left with nothing to do!

"MOMENTUM IS NOT SOMETHING THAT GOES AWAY IN AN INSTANT. MASTER THE ESSENCE OF SPEED TO CAPITALIZE ON IT. OTHERWISE, IT WILL PASS YOU BY AND EVEN ROLLOVER YOUR BODY."

DR BAK NGUYEN

Two weeks went by and I was like a lion in a cage! A lion! That started me on the path of the **LIONHEART**... **LEADERSHIP, Pandora's Box** was born. Twenty-one presidential speeches to empower each and every one of us to take our rightful place in the universe. Here's to summarize the book:

"Citizens of the world, we are all in it together, as a whole. As you bear more than your own weight, you have made a difference! And as you do so, you will soon be asking for more since it wasn't so hard..."

Three weeks later, I was out on top! Again, with ease and inspiration. I was more discreet about the second tome since the publishers had just started with the first one... I didn't want to burn too many steps all at once... But that's for the external appearances, inside, I was facing boredom, again. Inspiration was guiding me for the last two months, waking me up at 5 in the morning. We've grown side by side and just like that, we were back in our individual cages...

Three weeks in prison forced me to reflect on myself and what could come next. It's then, that I realized that I skipped a whole chapter! I started with *Entrepreneurship*, about how *to make things happened*. Then, it was **Leadership**, how to matter. In each of the tomes, I mentioned:

> "ONE'S STORY CAN ONLY BEGIN THE DAY
> ONE'S QUEST OF IDENTITY IS OVER."
>
> DR BAK NGUYEN

I have skipped **THE** *Quest of Identity*! A friend mentioned to me that it was easy for me since I got out of it, but people will need more than a few verses on the matter! He was absolutely right! I need to come back and finish the trilogy with a tome on the **Quest of Identity**. That matter is the broadest and will also be the hardest to cover since there are so many different paths.

We are citizens of the world.
Accept yourself to become a **lion**,
Believe in yourself enough

To fly your way into a **dragon**,
That animal which they say
Does not exist!

If you trust in yourself enough,
You will **break free**,
Free of the **template**,
Free of the **fear**,
Free to **fly**
And free **to be**!

Conquer, don't steal,
Seduce, don't lie,
Charm and be kind.

Freedom is the heart!
Power is the heart!
Destiny bows to the heart!

We started with one.
We found and added up
To become two and eight and ten
On our way to abundance.

Aim to be one!
The one, one whole, one unity,
Made of many.

Life is a circle,
We give and we take.
Life is given but not free.
Make sure to return
More than you took!

Destiny bows to the heart!

I wanted to build from the first two tomes and to look at the past with the strength of the future... but how? I didn't want to talk about my life again. I needed something more universal and, at the same time, intimate.

I had a lot of fun writing presidential speeches in **LEADERSHIP**. How to evolve from there? The answer came when a particular name hit me. It was like being rescued by a seal team, lead by the man who taught me my first words in English... John Lennon! I was out of the cage, once again!

What if John Lennon was still alive and, facing today's world political crisis, decided to stand in the public eye to run for prime minister? Not for himself, since he is dead and couldn't care less, but for our kind, for the whole, for each and every one of us and our future children!

"IDENTITY, THE ANTHOLOGY OF QUESTS."

That will be the third tome. Twenty-one themes of identity wrapped in presidential speeches, not aimed to move the crowds but aimed to help and to heal every member in those crowds. If all of us are ready to stand up for ourselves, leaders won't matter that much!

"THAT'S THE AMBITION AND THE LEGACY: TO EMPOWER EVERYONE!"

DR BAK NGUYEN

More than even **LEADERSHIP**, I need a medium that will make the content of these reflections available to all... The ambition is exactly what you are thinking: to *change the world* once more, but this time from **within**, from every single heart. The world starts with each individual and **IDENTITY**, Anthology of Quests will put you at the center.

You, whoever you are. You, where ever you are in your own quest of identity. You, each and every one of you, who are the base of our world. This book is about **ONE**, the beginning and the starting point.

Citizens of the world, aim to be one, the one, one whole, one unity, made of many. That's the anthology of life! Start with your one, find your unity and your legend will start. We are all small-minded people anyway! We need each other to be one! We need each other to be happy, so we, so you, so I, can be happy. This is the chorus of life. This is our song!

"LIFE IS A JOURNEY. THE QUEST OF IDENTITY
WAS ONLY THE BEGINNING!"
DR BAK NGUYEN

I'll say it again, don't make the journey harder than it has to be! Embrace it, learn from it, grow and enjoy every step of the way! You can either surf your destiny and feel the wind on your face or walk it, feeling each print you left behind. The choice is yours! Perfection? If you start **judging** now, your **only future is the past you are trying to polish** for the rest of time.

"POLISH IT AND IT WILL SHINE.
IT WILL UNFORTUNATELY NOT GROW
SINCE IT NOW LACKS LIFE!"
DR BAK NGUYEN

The problem started arising the day we started labeling. *Perfection* is exactly that, labeling, poisoning our heart and wasting our time. **Time** can be patient, but it will always be there to collect its due, with interests! You can run, flee, **Time** will eventually catch up with you. We are all **borrowers**, of life, of time, of talent. What do we have to lose? Why do we fear to lose something that is not even ours to begin with?

Stop being afraid, even better, cheat **Time** by sharing your experiences with the little ones! Fast track that youth to their own journey and you will have both cheated time and planted your legacy. The feeling is great, trust me!

"TO FEED IS NOT THE SAME THAN TO EAT!
SINCE ONE WILL GROW YOU AND THE OTHER WILL MAKE YOU FAT!
LIFE GOES BOTH WAYS!"

DR BAK NGUYEN

In the wild, *Life* is balanced. It's give and take. **Given but not free**. We need to bear more than our own weight to matter, to make a difference. And then, we will be asking for more.

We are, and will become what we eat. Whatever we ate, we absorb its energy and also its role in the universe. Whatever task has now fallen upon us! The more we see and understand *Life*, the harder it will be to simply eat and get fatter. So feed, **don't just eat**! Abundance is great, abundance is kind, abundance has to be earned. **Life is abundant, not free**.

"TRY TO SING A LIE, IT WILL SOUND JUST LIKE ONE! MUSIC IS EMOTION
AND EMOTION IS FROM THE HEART! ALL FILTERS ARE OFF!"

DR BAK NGUYEN

Sing, and the answer will come.
Sing, and the light will show.
Sing and even the pain will eventually fade away!

Make the most out of it!
Pain doesn't have to last forever.
Even ghosts have powers to master.

Evolve from it.
Sing your way through the darkness,
Through sadness,

Keep your heart opened
And **Happiness** will move back in,
Into a bigger heart, a **stronger heart**.

In the canvas, there are **no limits** but the one we set for ourselves. A template will help us start faster and with ease but the same template will also make it harder for us to really be ourselves, to find our unity and be whole. It is pretty easy to get lost in the canvas. Every time it will happen, sing, voice

66

yourself and listen to your emotions. They know the way to happiness since that was your *natural state*.

We will all face **the dive** one day. It's part of life, part of our destiny. Actually, it is the beginning of our journey. The *dive* will take courage, confidence, and determination to leave the known behind and to embrace the world of possibilities, the *unknown*.

The sooner the dive, the more time we will have for our *journey in the wild*. To each, our own quest. No judgment, since we all received different missions. We can choose to serve or not, our destiny will be written accordingly. Great or small, it is our choice!

"BREAK FREE FROM THE TEMPLATE TO FIND YOUR UNITY
AND START LIVING YOUR DESTINY!"

DR BAK NGUYEN

Remember that **Gratitude** is the only past with a future! Respect and honour what is given and make the most out of it! Don't judge anyone but yourself, respect your surroundings and **Time** will be on your side. In the wild, you are on your own, but you don't have to be alone! Open your heart and feel the *abundance of Life*. Open your heart to grow, to feed, to share and to shape *Life* into your vision.

> ## "TO HAVE A VISION IS TO DRAW THE HORIZON
> ## ON WHICH THE SUN WILL EVENTUALLY SET AND RISE."
> DR BAK NGUYEN

Trust in yourself, in your body, in your calling. In your quest for a cure, the past will have much to say, but no answer to give! Gratitude was the only past with a future! I cannot repeat it enough. Mark those words to save yourself. After all the pain, the roads, the adventures, one cannot afford to fall looking down at its feet and belly.

The answers are up and ahead, never down or behind. Emotions are the *chords of life*. To foresee the future, one has to master the chords first! Find your unity, trust your emotions and sing your song! Voice your passion and let Life be!

> ## "POWER IS WHAT WE CALL THE INSECURITY OF ONE TO MATTER."
> DR BAK NGUYEN

Love is sweetness and bitterness all at once. It is the first and the kindest lesson of life since it does not aim to protect us but rather to prepare us for what is to come. After love, the most common quest is the **Quest for Power**.

Keep pride and power far from your heart and you'll do just fine. If you want to succeed every single time, turn your **liability into leverage**! Act on your thoughts and make your way to abundance and peace! Fight for what's in your heart and for the little ones. Lend a hand when possible, the best **wins are the one against time**!

We have much to do, to taste, to accomplish. We don't need the guilt, we need the conscience to remember that our purpose was greater than ourselves. To matter, we need each other!

That's the **Anthology of Life**! That's your destiny. Make it great, make it whole, make it matter. Believe in yourself and embrace the possibilities of life. Life is greater than each of us. If you let it guide you, you'll be walking your destiny.

This is mine, may it inspires you to yours. This is the **POWER OF YES**, volume one. Welcome to the **Alphas**.

SOMEONE BETTER,
SOMEONE STRONGER,
SOMEONE HUNGRIER,
I BECAME MORE.
DR BAK NGUYEN.

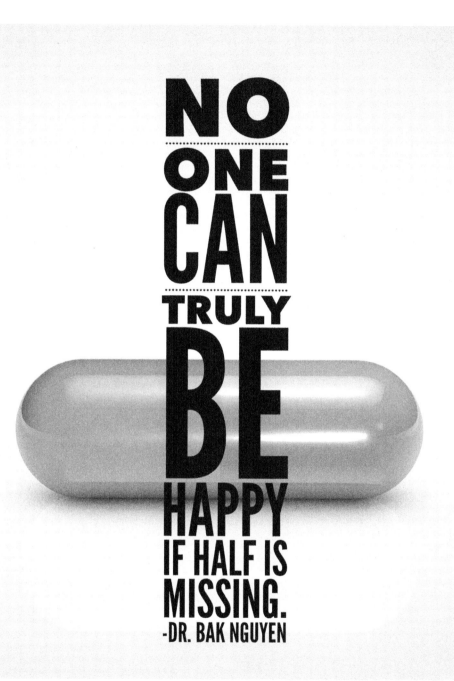

NO
ONE
CAN
TRULY
BE
HAPPY
IF HALF IS
MISSING.
-DR. BAK NGUYEN

CHAPTER 4

PROFESSION HEALTH

JANUARY 2018

BY DR BAK NGUYEN

"IN OUR RANKS, ELITE IS AVERAGE, AND HUMILITY,
A STANDARD. BUT WE ARE STILL HUMAN!"
DR BAK NGUYEN

Usually, heroes and champions stand isolated
Since there are so few of them.
We are legions of good
Sharing our science and unique drive.

We are a community sharing knowledge and recipes,
Spreading Hope all around the world.
Why can't we be a community
Taking care of our own?

This is the beginning of a new era, one where we *reconcile* our *fears* and our *joy*; our *skills* and our *feelings*; an era where we are finally accepted for what we are: *champions marathoners*, every day's *heroes, white coats*.

We have gone so far, done so much, sacrifice for so long to miss out on happiness. Yes, we are the *Elite Forces of Good* and we are humans. It is that humanity that gives the warmth of hope to our patients, not the whiteness of our coat. We may be the elite but we are not perfect. We may be heavily trained but we still have to learn every day.

We found our worth serving others, healing and giving hope. Our Profession trained us to be confident and strong since our patients will feed on that confidence to gain trust in our treatments.

"TO BELIEVE IS THE FIRST STEP TO WIN, TO HEAL."

DR BAK NGUYEN

It's been two weeks since the completion of my fourth book, **IDENTITY, Anthology of Quests**. I gave it all I had! This last one was particularly demanding since it was aimed for the largest of public, literally everyone! I will resist the temptation to unveil the secret of Identity here, but let me say:

"YOU ARE NOT ALONE AND YOU DON'T HAVE TO BE. BUT MARK MY WORDS, YOU ARE ON YOUR OWN!"
DR BAK NGUYEN

As the last words of **Identity** went into bytes, I knew that it wasn't over, that the rest was just for a few days... I've promised my 7 years old son, William Bak, to write with him the **LEGEND** of the **CHICKEN**, the **LION** and the **DRAGON HEART**.

Easy, I thought... All I had to do is to select chapters from my previous books, throw the concepts at him and record what will come out of his mouth, in 7 years old's dialect. This should be a walk in the park! I couldn't be more mistaken!

To write for children is way more complex than I've ever imagined. To keep their attention for a long time is a challenge for the divine. To make sense of all of it and to capture it with appeal will definitely take much, much more time and energy than first anticipated. And I was in for three volumes!!!

That's how 2018 started for me. Not quite. As I was writing **LEADERSHIP**, many of my close friends and allies were wondering why I was writing about politic and leadership while my own profession, doctors, dentists, white coats and all the people in the health sector could benefit from my unique views and takes.

As I finished **LEADERSHIP** and then, **IDENTITY**, I knew that **PROFESSION HEALTH, the Unconventional Quest for Happiness** would be around the corner.

So I cheated! I took notes separately as I wrote the two last tomes and was promising myself to look at them later. Between the texts of **eHappyPedia**, the reflections of **LEADERSHIP** and the constant repositioning of **IDENTITY**, the path of **PROFESSION HEALTH** was clarifying by itself, one quest at a time.

I am addicted to my own momentum, that you already knew. Since the beginning of my career as an author, the words just flew from my thoughts and shaping themselves as they filled the chapters.

After two weeks building the spine of the children's trilogy, I needed some distraction from being a co-author to my 7 years old son. Not to mention the pressure I had to write for my own people, my colleagues, people I knew and worked with!

"YOU CANNOT POUR MUCH FROM AN EMPTY CUP!"

Most of us had given up much to earn our white coat, our stripes, our scrubs. We gave it everything we had to be part of the art of life, of giving, again and again, giving our best on a daily basis! We are strong, we are resilient, we are committed! That was part of the selection process! But how much more can we give it our best, repeatedly?

Doctors, nurses, assistants, clerks, esteem colleagues, I thank you for your dedication and continued service to others! We are part of the bigger picture, the whole. We bear more than our own weight and we make the difference on a daily basis. Only to do it again after a short night sleep!

"IF WE ARE MEASURED BY THE SIZE OF OUR HEART, WE ARE AMONG THE HEAVY LEAGUE!"

DR BAK NGUYEN

This book, these reflections are for you, all for you. As you have given your best, your all every day, I will pour in here, all that I have gathered and comprehend within my last twenty years in our profession. Since my first days in dental school, I had to rejuvenate my passion, to generate time and love to devote myself to others. Now, I am empowering you with my secrets and recipes. You have earned much, may this help you ease your way to happiness as a permanent state of mind, as a permanent state of heart.

I am pleased to introduce to you a colleague who joined **Mdex** recently: Dr Mirjana Sindolic. Dr Sindolic has been teaching paediatric dentistry for the last two decades. A sharp mind, a soft touch and most of all, a sensitive heart, Dr Sindolic will be sharing with us her wisdom and her secret to connect with our patients and ourselves.

Professor Robert Durand, DMD, MSc, professor at *University of Montreal*, Faculty of Dental Medicine, will also be among the contributors to the reflection of our profession. Together, we cumulate more than 75 years of professional experiences in serving, healing and connecting on a daily basis. It's a real honour to have friends and colleagues of that caliber joining in this endeavour.

Other than the main collaborators, I am honoured to report great names like Dr Jean De Serres, former chairman of *Hema-Quebec* and former teacher at *McGill University*, Faculty of Medicine, Counsel-Minister Luis Kalaff Sanchez will be joining the conversation. Other contributors are Dr Miguel Russo, MD, and bankers Anthony Siggia and Kyle Ives. At this stage, we are all joining forces to explore solutions to the burnout rate, depression and suicide affecting our members, white coats.

To heal the world, we must start by healing ourselves. And healing we need. The first step is to admit that we need help, ourself. That's TOME ONE of this trilogy, the diagnosis. Reviewing this book with my colleague, Dr Sindolic, we realized that there was so much to say and to share that within one volume, it was impossible to make sense of all of it. This is what we've figured out:

1- DIAGNOSIS, 2- TREATMENT, 3- REEVALUATION

In science as in Medicine, we start with phase 1, **DIAGNOSIS**, **A HYPOTHESIS**. Even if we can never be 100% certain of our diagnosis, we make educated guesses and try to come up with the best course of action fitting our *Diagnosis* and *hypothesis*. Then, we focus on the treatment, tunnel vision on the causes we think are responsible and plan the operation.

In phase 2, **TREATMENT**, we become *blindsided* by anything but our *hypothesis*. it's not a flaw, it's the design of the process. Mainly, in the treatment phase, we carve out the cause of our problem.

In phase 3, **REEVALUATION**, we go back in, with an opened and critical spirit to find out what went well and what when wrong. If it went well, what did succeed? Were we just lucky? If it went wrong, what did we missed? Where were the flaws in our thinking or execution?

PROFESSION HEALTH is about the *diagnosis*, phase 1. I will take centre stage to bring some light on the matter, to illustrate to each of us, the urgency to act, to break the curse of isolation before it is too late. I'll do things, the only way I know how to do them, with conviction, impact and passion. This is a matter of national security since, we, white coats, are responsible for the wellbeing of all the others.

We gave it all to be a white coat, to stay commit and to give our best day in and day out for months, years, even decades. We do it with dignity and excellence without any room for failure. That's just impossible, the odds and the stats are all stacked against us, but we do it anyway. In every other field, we call those trays the marks of **champions**. We, we called it *average*.

And then, we go out, giving our best, not to better ourself but to help others. Each day, putting the needs of the other before our own. From all cultures across time and space, these are the marks of **heroes** and often, the heroes were punctual, not daily. We, we call it *average*.

And again, we do not talk about it out of respect, out of *oath*. **Humility** in all cultures throughout history is the nature of greatness and goodness. We, we call it doing our job! Do we need help? At least some recognition. We are white coats, selected from the best, heavily trained and chosen to receive the power to heal and the authority to care.

"NO ONE CAN BE TRULY HAPPY IF HALF IS MISSING."

DR BAK NGUYEN

This endeavour is a safe place for us, all of us, white coats to open ourselves up. We badly need and to retake control over our life and our happiness. Even when everything seems fine, we all know what we chose to bury deep down.

Before and after wearing that white coat, we were and will be someone. Someone with love, fears, feelings, and desire. That part, we have buried too deep to the point of forgetting its existence. That's not healing, its straight amputation and denial. No one can reach perfection with only half of him or herself.

We are part science, part human.
To be whole is our chance for happiness.
Before getting into med, dental, medical science schools,

We all experienced that insecurity
Of looking at the profession from the outside
With envy, with high hopes,
Thinking how perfect the world is

On the other side of the glass.
There was no sale's pitch,
Just the noble feeling of goodness
To heal the world and to do good.

People were either smiling or crying.
Smiling from the release of their burden
Or crying for another chance for *Life*.

The image is strong,
The emotions are real,
We all believed in it.
Most of us still do.

As we are looking from the other side of the glass, our hearts started to beat as never we felt before. We see the nobility of the profession. "That's what I want to do!" Both inspired and intimidated, we stepped back for a minute, our eyes looking in from the outside of the glass. But then, something magical happened, we saw our reflection in the glass, our face layered on top of the profession, the nobility.

Like falling in love, that was our calling. That heartbeat will never really leave us. We will go back to our books and give them our best shot, our best efforts, energies, our youth, the entirety of our hopes. The sleepless nights, all the beautiful Saturday afternoon volunteering instead of partying, the countless proofs we will have to accumulate before we can finally submit our candidacy to join the *Elite Forces of Good*.

And when the day comes, each of us knows too well the feeling of insecurity, opening that letter from the admission committee... those minutes before opening the envelope has left an imprint that all of us carry around since. Some has exploded of joy, some will, later on, having to prove their worth for another year... I've been there and you've been there too. That feeling of insecurity, of hope, of acceptance, of determination, are what our white coats stand upon.

We are all here today because we were there once. But inside, the same calling that once pushed us on our feet to walk our path is now the theme of our heartbeat. It never left, we only became used to it. From the flame of passion and the light of hope, we have become one with our profession.

"THERE IS NO GLASS ANYMORE TO SEE THE NOBILITY OF OUR COMMITMENT AND, AT THE SAME TIME, OUR FACES FROM THE REFLECTION."

DR BAK NGUYEN

I am with you, wearing my white coat. Busy by the minutes and always running to my next *saving the day*. Believe it or not, it is the same feeling, the same calling. We all share the same DNA and the oxytocin's level is running pretty high in our kind: the student, the doctor, the foreigner. We are one, we are a community having to take care of our own, of ourselves.

84

This is my cry for help, for hope. Not for myself, but for all of us. Let's stop comparing the stars on our shoulders and the medals slowing us down. Let's stop pretending that we do not feel, that we are stronger and that everything is all right. Things are not that bad when we are deflecting. Oh yes, we are deflecting, we know all too well how to leverage on our profession to take care of others while ignoring our own needs and feelings.

> "THIS IS NOT THE END OF THE JOURNEY, MERELY THE BEGINNING OF A NEW ERA, AN ERA OF JOY AND HOPE."
>
> DR BAK NGUYEN

I thank Professor Durand to have embraced this project with enthusiasm and to have accepted to build from the ground up a research project between the *University of Montreal*, the *Canadian Government* and the **Mdex**'s Group to better understand the causes of depression and suicidal thoughts among white coats, especially dentists.

On the matter, I formally take the engagement to have my part of the proceeds from the sale of this book, **PROFESSION HEALTH** to fund a foundation financing that research for the future years. You are all welcomed to participate.

For as long as we have the support of the *Canadian Government*, each dollar invested will be matched by the Government. This is my contribution to our profession, my way of expressing my Gratitude to a profession who has embraced me as one of their own.

I invite you to join the movement and to open up to share. To share your secrets of how you made it, to share your feelings of satisfaction but also of insecurities and how you coped with them. To connect with brothers and sisters sharing the same addiction to oxytocin, to the hormone of sympathy, of warmth.

We are the past, the present, and the future. We gave it our best, every day, never backing down. We are champions. We put the needs of others before our own, time and time again until it became a primary nature. We are heroes. We do it without much recognition, we do not even think about recognition. We are white coats, excellence is our average. We are the *perfect hybrids of science and humanity*.

We owe it to ourselves to be happy and to take care of each other, not just our patients, but our peers, our brothers and sisters in arms. We are a community and together we stand tall. We must, if we want to stand a chance to last, not just as individuals but as a profession, as the *Elite Forces for Good* and *Hope* to the world.

Believe in yourself and embrace the possibilities of life. Life is greater than each of us. If you let it guide you, you'll be walking your destiny.

This is mine, may it inspires you to yours. This is the **POWER OF YES**, volume one. Welcome to the **Alphas**.

SOMEONE BETTER,
SOMEONE STRONGER,
SOMEONE HUNGRIER,
I BECAME MORE.
DR BAK NGUYEN.

A DISRUPTOR IS AN ENTREPRENEUR WHO HAS ESTABLISHED A NEW BENCHMARK.

There will be a before and after era.

•••

Dr. Bak Nguyen

CHAPTER 5

INDUSTRIES

DISRUPTORS

APRIL-MAY 2018

BY DR BAK NGUYEN

Eight months have passed since I started taking the path to write and share my thoughts with you, I now have six books to show. Actually, the fifth one is still pending since I am waiting for the respond of guest authors to join in. I hope to wrap the fifth instalment, **PROFESSION HEALTH** within the next month.

Writing with others has its pros and cons. On the con's side, surely the waiting is something new to me. In all my past endeavours, I was wrapping them within a month, keeping the momentum going. Waiting isn't one of my strong suits! But the rewards, sharing with my co-authors and guest authors is such a rich experience, not just in knowledge but also as a vibe of positive energy.

"ALONE, THERE'S JUST SO MUCH WE CAN DO."

DR BAK NGUYEN

Eight months, six books, one big opening of **Mdex & Co**, my new concept revolutionizing the dental industry with a philosophy of sharing, of happiness, of intelligence and of sustainable development, we are rocking the world, in a good way!

The launch and the interviews brought me to a new level of awareness and business networking. Three weeks later, I was giving my first panel as an **INDUSTRY DISRUPTOR** at the *John*

Molson School of Business, part of *Concordia University* in Montreal.

> ## "A DISRUPTOR IS AN ENTREPRENEUR WHO HAS ESTABLISHED A NEW BENCHMARK. THERE WILL BE A BEFORE, AND AFTER ERA."
>
> DR BAK NGUYEN

I did not realize the full weight of those words right away. To be called a *disruptor* is a promotion from my previous function, entrepreneur, a recognition of my vision to change the future of an entire industry. I humbly took the stage and delivered the only way I knew how to be: being myself, totally myself.

I shared that panel with two titan entrepreneurs, Jamie Benizri, a lawyer and disruptor who is bringing technology and democracy to the conservatives law institutions and industry. Jamie is a builder of networks and relationships, he bridges the future by bringing people together. He does not fight with boxing gloves but with finest and the style of a diplomat smiling to get people to his view.

Lennie Moreno is a serial entrepreneur at his core, rapping and singing his philosophy and his will to reform the solar industry. Yes, you read right, a poet writing the new rules of the solar energy industry. From different paths of life, from totally different industries, we came together on stage, learning to share the spotlight and trying to stay civilized…

94

Prior to the panel, some of the producers told me to bring my A-game. Those co-panelists are heavyweight and they do not take prisoners. I will need to fight my way through for my voice to have a chance. Usually, from a panel, only one shall stand tall... Well, the only thing I knew was to be myself and hope for the best...

We nailed it, totally! The crowd was asking for more, even after nearly 90 minutes of non-stop exchange. They were empowered and the hopes from their eyes filled the entirety of the conference room. On stage, we learned, Jamie, Lennie and I to know each other and to gain the respect of one another.

It was not diplomacy, it was *synergy*, the kind of vibe you feel being part of a football team winning the finals! That's exactly what it was! Exhilarating for each of us and for every single member in the crowd. We became friends. I kept contact with Jamie after the event.

This is where my life took another turn, a 90-degree turn! This is where my friend Thierry, the producer of the speaking event, introduced me to Casey Neistat, the Super YOU TUBER star. I told you the story already, I had a hard time connecting and relating to Casey. But after a while listening to him, I notice how he succeed compare to me. He and I have creativity, the big difference is that I was being cheap about it!

At that stage, I just received the response of three of the biggest publishers in Quebec saying that they liked my book, the french version of **SYMPHONY OF SKILLS**, but it wasn't a good fit for their market. To be rejected is always hard, but to have to wait three months for that answer was the hardest on my spirit. I can write three books within that time!

That day, I took two major decisions listening to Casey. Like Casey, I will be generous about my creativity. Every time he finished a video, he put it up on YOUTUBE unless he had a better alternative. He didn't care much about what will happen to that video or how much money he will be making out of it, he simply posts his video and moves on to his next project, always giving his best.

I am writing books, I need my "YOUTUBE" which is called **AMAZON**. That how I started to push for my book. My job is to write books, not to sell them. I write and put them on **AMAZON** and move on to the next.

Easier said than done. Publishing books is an expertise on itself and demand skills and mastery. Until today, I have successfully put only one of my books online. I am still working towards a more efficient solution to have them available as fast as possible. My next stop is **Apple Books**. The simple fact that I got inspired by Casey, my career as a writer went to new heights.

The second thing that I decided that day was to embrace the **YESMAN's** challenge to reset my mind and to open up to the world of possibilities. I promised myself to be open for 12 months and to meet and greet whoever was willing to shake hands with me. I put my money where my words were right away! The birth of this book is a direct result of it!

Today, I am honoured to present to you my new endeavour and 6th instalment, **INDUSTRIES DISRUPTOR** sharing my experience as an entrepreneur and how I pulled it through to be recognized. I'll be sharing feelings and knowledge.

Growing and evolving through the process, I will nurture and breed the positive vibe we felt on stage for a brief moment. I am the one writing this book, but sharing a positive vibe with other entrepreneurs kickstarted the idea.

"THE VIBE OF POSITIVITY IS SUSTAINABLE
AS WE KEEP SHARING AND GROWING."
DR BAK NGUYEN

Good vibe attracts good people! Exchanging and networking with Jamie's friends, I met with James Stephan-Usypchuk. James is the founder of JSU solutions, the #1 Facebook advertising agency in Canada. Titles do not bear much weight with me, but within a month, our conversation brought both of us to a new level. Strategy, marketing, philosophy, James is from a league of his own. He is surely a *disruptor* in his high pace industry.

James is an inspiration. To understand a mind like his, and to capture part of his science are, in my opinion, the key to launch, and to run any contemporary business or endeavour.

To write a book with such high energy people, with entrepreneurs who do not stop and ask for permission, who have the habit to write the rules instead of kneeling to them is a great opportunity but also a great challenge. How do we keep the cohesion without compromising? From each of us, Jamie, James and myself, we need to be genuine, to exchange and to disclose the bottom line. That's what worth your time and ours.

I extended the invitation to another great friend of mine, banker Rouba Sakr, one of the bankers who allowed the launch of **Mdex & Co**. Rouba is a passionate and loyal banker who made it possible for a disruptor as myself, to build and take over the world, for the better!

Rouba has the keys to make it happen. If you are wondering how we do it, Rouba has first-hand experience and knowledge of bridging the entrepreneur vision and passion with the numbers that bankers will embrace, or at least tolerate.

If anything, I just delivered to you one of my greatest recipe for success, my bankers! For the first time, entrepreneurs and bankers will disclose the dance they entertain to rewrite the existence and drive our world to new heights!

This will be the second time that Rouba and I shared a stage. At the Olympic Stadium, we shared our story of *love and hate*, the story between a Disruptor and a Banker. At the Olympic Stadium, we nailed it, since Bankers rarely have the chance to talk about their point of view and their experience behind the curtains, trying to materialize the much-needed resources to support entrepreneurs and *industries disruptors*.

"SHOOT FOR THE MOON, THAT'S THE BEST WAY
TO MINIMIZE THE RISK-REWARD RATIO."

DR BAK NGUYEN

I wrote my part of **INDUSTRIES DISRUPTORS** within a little more than a week, surfing from my *momentum*. Rouba joined in the vibe and delivered shortly after. We are still waiting for Jamie and James to find the time in their busy schedule to join and share their experiences and wisdom. I usually do not wait, ever, but this time, the wait is worth since both Jamie and James will bring their unique perspectives to this endeavour.

You see, when you are creating and implementing something new, you believe in a vision, in thin air. There is no recipe for success and everything is an opinion until it is done. In other words, your views are what matter the most since you believe in something that does not exist yet!

The stronger you believe, the better are your chances of seeing your vision materialize. I did it in the dental industry, but to have in a same book, how Jamie did it in the legal industry and James, in the ever-changing world of digital marketing, we should be able to find some common threads as baselines.

I have nothing but respect for entrepreneurs, any entrepreneurs, no matter their level of success. To be an entrepreneur is to refuse to bow down to inertia and inefficiency. Often, the same people you are trying to help are the one resistant to the change, the solution.

> " THE PAIN MUST BE GREATER THAN THE PAIN OF CHANGE
> TO ALLOW ANY CHANGE TO BE ACCEPTED."
>
> DR BAK NGUYEN

The pain of change, that's a subject I covered in my first book, **SYMPHONY OF SKILLS**. It is just funny how far it is already in my mind, but also how true and present is the concept in the real world. With much time, failures and some wins, what I can tell you is that to last as an entrepreneur, you must love your mission and the people. Those who are in it for the money, the fame or a quick rise will all experience the burns soon enough.

But to those who are entrepreneurs, the real ones, those looking to bring a good change in this world, please do not back down. We all breathe the same air and drink the same water, but our outcome had to be different. Believe in yourself and your vision, connect with other entrepreneurs just for the fun of connecting, of breaking the isolation, to have a chance to catch your breath before you dive right back in.

> "DON'T ASK YOUR MENTOR WHAT THEY THINK,
> ASK THEM HOW THEY WOULD DO IT, EVEN IF THEY DISAGREE!"
> DR BAK NGUYEN

Entrepreneurs, please accept my gift to each of you. Be bold enough to have complete faith in your vision and be humble enough to keep an open mind to learn from other people who won the race before you. If you are inventing something new, you must put all the chances on your side, don't take unnecessary risks. In other words, forget pride and do not try to recreate the wheel, you will be setting yourself up for failure.

Even if you are a *leader* and a *disruptor*, choose your battles carefully and learn from the bests to have a chance to touch the finished line. At our level, it's not just the fact that we tried that is important, but also that we had a fair chance to win. Forget about your pride and choose your battle. This is one of the *key ingredients* of my rise.

For 20 years I have fought my way through, but lately, I started scoring win after win. I owe each of my wins to my openness to learn from other industries and how I choose my battles. Take this gift and the sooner you'll understand it and apply it, the better will be your *chances of success*. And since you'll start connecting and sharing with like-minded people, you'll be raising your happiness level at the same occasion.

> ## "TO SUCCEED, ONE NEEDS TO OPEN. TO LAST, ONE NEEDS TO HAVE FUN."
> DR BAK NGUYEN

Believe in yourself and embrace the possibilities of life. Life is greater than each of us. If you let it guide you, you'll be walking your destiny.

This is mine, may it inspires you to yours. This is the **POWER OF YES**, volume one. Welcome to the **Alphas**.

SOMEONE BETTER,
SOMEONE STRONGER,
SOMEONE HUNGRIER,
I BECAME MORE.
DR BAK NGUYEN.

102

MAKE
IT HAPPEN!
-DR. BAK NGUYEN

CHAPTER 6

CHANGING THE WORLD
FROM A DENTAL CHAIR

MAY 2018

BY DR BAK NGUYEN

Lately, between the opening of **Mdex & Co**, the launching of my speaking career, the books, things are great and moving at a crazy pace.

In the midst of the effervescence, it was a great surprise and honour to receive the nomination for "**Ernst and Young, Entrepreneur of the Year**". As I got through the first rounds of interviews with the EY selection committee, a clear sense of humility and hope was in the air, from all the parties in the room.

As an entrepreneur, I live up to my title as *Industries Disruptor*, a title given to me as I took the stage for the first time at the *John Molson School of Business*. But as an **EY nominee**, I am just starting my disruption record; things make a lot of sense, but still, have to be proven.

In medicine, most medical acts happen outside of an operating room. In dental, most of the acts occur inside of an operating room. Why is that? That's the primary question that I raised as I started building **Mdex & Co**.

Today, our first "pilot" modern dental complex has been completed, secured and financed, I may add. We went a long way since the beginning of the journey. **Mdex & Co** is made of three main branches:

- **Mdex & Co**, the "hotel" concept changing the way we will go to the dentist, drastically improving the experience for both the dentist and the patient.

- **Mdex V**, the dedicated and customized dental platform. I like to call it our Operation System. Securing and bringing the business and the professionals closer to their clientele. We worked hard to remove unnecessary filters between the dentist and his patients and reducing the need for phone calls, dated from last century's practice. **Mdex V** will be a platform opening the dental field to many more expertises such as affordable legal and financing services at the fingertips of dentists.

- **Mdex Industries**, the engineering division. We have built from the ground up new ways to build a dental clinic, reducing the need of drilling and reducing our imprint on the environment by nearly 70%, and our imprint on the building to close to nothing. The dental field has now joined the sustainable growth mentality.

Each one of those branches has a separate business plan and aims for different markets, but they all come together to shape the vision of **Mdex**: *to change the world from a dental chair*! I had much support and financial vouching, different interests from institutional investors such as the *FTQ funds*, I even managed to monopolize the attention of a high ranking officer of the *Caisse de Dépôt* - their number 3, I've been told -

for more than an hour and a half. Yes, the idea and the fundamentals are great!

> ## "UNTIL IT IS DONE, IT IS STILL AIR! GOOD AIR, BUT STILL A CONCEPT IN THE MAKING."
>
> DR BAK NGUYEN

I can prove each one of the facts that I mentioned and have the track record to prove that I walk my talk, even if I talk a lot... But as we went through the selection process, the judges started to share friendly advices with me. They love the vision, embrace the vibe but I still need to make up for the fact that my project is at its launch! That's what I have to make up for: my launch!

It is both the tipping point of my whole career as a dentist and visionary, but also what can break or make me! I still need to bring my ideas to the market and make sure that people understand our concept as quickly as possible.

> ## "BY THE END OF THE DAY, BUSINESS IS COMMUNICATION."
>
> DR BAK NGUYEN

The **EY nomination** came as a blessing from the sky. I am very conscious of my weak ankle: my thin financial past as **Mdex & Co** since my project is at its birth. In this book, I will make up for my startup status by sharing with you my vision of the future, and by disclosing to you most of my present and daily wins. Not just logic and numbers, but the true story behind **Mdex & Co**, the making of a company, its philosophy, and its leverage.

This book will be written based on the list of questions that **EY**'s judges had to go through with every single nominee. Within those pages, you will read what, why and how, a dentist has started to change the world from a dental chair. I surely hope that it will make up for the thin past of my newborn company.

"A DISRUPTOR IS AN ENTREPRENEUR WHO HAS ESTABLISHED A NEW BENCHMARK. THERE WILL BE A BEFORE AND AFTER ERA."

DR BAK NGUYEN

I am in the middle of writing **INDUSTRIES DISRUPTORS** with my co-author Jamie Benizri who has also received the same EY nomination. *Industries disruptors*, that was the title with which I started my career as a speaker for *Influence Gen* at the *John Molson School of Business, Concordia University*. That's where I met Jamie, as a co-panelist.

Our friendship started on stage, as we were empowering the crowd of young entrepreneurs and future disruptors. Right after the panel, we wanted to keep the positive vibe going, and Jamie and I agreed to join forces to write a book together about how we each have impacted our respective industry.

As we kept close contact after the *Influence Gen* event at the *John Molson School of Business*, we grew our friendship exponentially, at a frenetic pace. What do I like about the man? We do share the same vibe, the same level of crazy high energy, and to top it, we both thrive by empowering other people! We were like the mirror image of each other!

"IF I WAS A DENTIST, I WOULD BE YOU!"
JAMIE BENIZRI

As we met for a business meeting that day, he came in a little late. His justification was that he had to pass by the **EY**'s offices to shoot his Instagram story: announcing his nomination as *EY Entrepreneur of the Year*. I was pretty happy for him, but in the back of my mind, I was wondering if he was making too much noise around the first step of a long journey! I kept my opinion to myself and asked him: "How can I help to make it happen?"

He laughed and thanked me for my support. Two weeks later, as I finally opened my email box, I had an email from EY. I was a nominee too! I was already feeling great with my new promotion as *"Industries Disruptor"*. Imagine my feelings when I received my nomination! The exact words were:

CONGRATULATIONS, YOU HAVE BEEN NOMINATED...

ERNST AND YOUNG

And then it hit me: in his Instagram videos, Jamie was just using those exact words from **EY**'s selection committee, nothing more and nothing less! Oscar nominees run with their title for years, if not for their whole career! Thus I learned from Jamie and started my communication on the social media with the mention that I was now a nominee of **EY**.

As a doctor, I am shaped a little square, and usually will not say a word until "thank you", or until I am quietly dropped. In the case of the second advent, not too many people would have learned about the embarrassment... In the present case, it's an honour just to make the cut to the nomination board!

Now it is for me to *make it happen*, to show my true nature as an entrepreneur from the get-go! Let's make the most out of both the nomination and the journey! So I started sharing on the web.

Things exploded on my social media within hours. It gave a meaning to most of the events in both my life and Jamie's. We were preparing to speak together at the Olympic Stadium later that Spring; from then, the communication went around two *EY nominees for Entrepreneur of the year* joining forces, for a book, for conferences, namely, wherever it mattered! Our brand was suddenly set! **Disruptors and Nominees**!

Then I agreed with him that no matter who would win, we would keep our relationship intact and make the most out of this journey! Meanwhile, I had a diplomatic mission to fly to; on the way, while waiting at the airport, a crazy idea came up: "Let's make a challenge and stop by every *Ernst and Young's* offices on the way, just to say hi!"

I filmed myself with a selfie, talking about the idea while waiting at the airport. I posted it online just before taking off. Now it was real! Miami was my first stop, dropping by **EY**'s offices, unannounced and asking for a tour on-camera... To be honest, I can meet with ministers and generals, presidents and bankers, but dropping by unannounced was a little awkward to me! They welcomed us with open arms! What a relief. The first challenge completed, the video went online and went on fire!

"It's up to me to make it happen!" That's what I told myself! "Now that it's fun, I will double down on the endeavour and the audacity. Always, respectfully and with class!" This is how the idea to write this book arrived on the table!

I was scratching my head to figure out how I could make my case within 10 minutes in front of the judges. "They will only read what is on paper and feel the vibe of 10 minutes of a hard cold business pitch. Even if I can speak crazy fast, there is just so much they could have from my story and vision within 10 minutes, and I would look in a hurry, losing both my charisma and nomination..."

So I decided to go the other way around! I would try to use as fewer words as possible, to appear calm and ready to listen and receive their comments. I was going to let my work speak for itself: I would present a signed copy of a book written especially for the occasion, giving the judges an in-depth sight of who *Dr Bak* is and what he is trying to accomplish. Even if all they saw and touched was the cover of the book, the judges would at least have the feeling of meeting with a genuine and true entrepreneur! Maybe even understand his disruptive title...

It's not up to me to decide if I win or not. But I still can put all the odds in my favour! This journey has already brought me out of my comfort zone. To have less than a month to write a book and have it published was a challenge that I was a little insecure about...

Usually, when I write, it's about the past and what I've done. To write in present tense, almost in real-time, surely differs from what I know. I will enjoy this journey, meet with as many interesting people as possible and grow from this! Maybe with a new title by the end of it...

"IT'S CRAZY WHAT YOU CAN DO WHEN YOU ARE EMPOWERED!"

DR BAK NGUYEN

I have exceeded my own expectations writing this book in five days, on top of my crazy schedule. Five days ago, it was humanly impossible. Can you imagine that now I am ahead of schedule? Not by much, but still ahead of schedule! This is the perfect image of my career and of the story of **Mdex**: things we thought impossible were made possible, not by magic, but through dedication and passion.

If you asked me, never would I have told you that within two years, I would have brought to life three different companies, upgraded an industry into the new millennium and become a champion of the environment, writing seven books and becoming a speaker on top of that.

And if I would have planned all of this, which I didn't, I would not have accomplished it since I would have been too busy planning to listen to the real needs and pains of the market. And my books would have been vain.

So if I could change anything, would I? I guess not, since everything is connected and I am the compound effect of everything happening to me. It all leads to this exact moment: the present, writing with my words and my thoughts, the future.

I know that my plans are solid and that we have an aiming force that can reach for the moon. I am also very aware of the downfalls and the risks associated with my launch. I am not taking anything lightly...

"LOYALTY IS TO A COMMITMENT, NOT TO A PERSON."

DR BAK NGUYEN

Just like this nomination, being a nominee is a huge honour in itself. Taking this nomination seriously brought me to the next level: this book and everything coming with it! Going through the **EY** questions seemed simple at first as I got through them in the interviews with the judges of the first round, in front of the camera with my team, and then going through them again while writing.

Meanwhile, I was meeting with potential business partners and investors for **Mdex & Co**. I was just bathing into **Mdex**'s story. Thanks to that, the meetings went more than well, and the first email I got back was: « You are impressive... »

So if you asked me what I've learned in the process, I would tell you: to just *make it happen*.

"IF YOU CAN THINK OF IT, DO IT!"
DR BAK NGUYEN

I guess I was always like that, but today, I've learned to trust my instincts and to jump headfirst. Not for a dare, but because I know that I have it in me to *make it happen*! That's the key phrase of this book! *Make it happen*! So if I could talk to my younger self, I would tell him just that: *make it happen*! And do it now!

"THIS IS MY LIFE! EVERY MOMENT COUNTS!"
DR BAK NGUYEN

And about the future? I know that **Mdex & Co** will be a household name, an Industry leader and a game-changer. I also know that the amount of work, intelligence, and dedication left ahead is at an insanely crazy level! But this book proved to me that nothing is really impossible.

Really, momentum!
Momentum by sharing,
Momentum by inspiring,

Momentum by doing,
Momentum by reaching out,
Momentum by saying yes!

The future growth is insane! The potential to do good and to capture the market is simply so in our favour that it's hard to believe. And since it might be hard to believe, test it! I won't waste my time thinking about something that is hard to believe, I'll try it and then I'll know!

I'm still in the process of surviving my launch and the transition period, but the hopes are high and so is the energy in the air! I am finishing my final thoughts at the counter of a great restaurant in the Toronto Harbor: Amsterdam Brewery.

Can you believe that I am writing these words while waiting for my pizza to arrive? Make the most of what's available and make it happen. Thank you for the opportunity, thank you for the journey.

If you'll excuse me, I need to get to the Air Canada Center to meet with a boxing champion defending his title. I've been invited by his team to explore ways to collaborate on a book together. Maybe I'll be starting my eighth book by tomorrow? Who knows?

Believe in yourself and embrace the possibilities of life. Life is greater than each of us. If you let it guide you, you'll be walking your destiny.

This is mine, may it inspires you to yours. This is the **POWER OF YES**, volume one. Welcome to the **Alphas**.

SOMEONE BETTER,
SOMEONE STRONGER,
SOMEONE HUNGRIER,
I BECAME MORE.
DR BAK NGUYEN.

ON THIN ICE, SPEED UP. THAT'S HOW YOU WILL EVENTUALLY LEARN TO FLY!

—DR. BAK NGUYEN

CHAPTER 7

MOMENTUM TRANSFER
AUGUST 2018

BY DR BAK NGUYEN

MOMENTUM is more than a word or a concept, a *Momentum* is a way to gather the energy within and to concentrate it into a focal point. From that focal point, you are building the **EYE** of your *Tornado*. To start, you need to believe in something greater than yourself and to have enough confidence to believe that you can withstand the doubt and negativity.

Just like in warfare, the victory is to those who **believe the strongest, the longest**. This is not about war, it is about gaining enough time to build power around an idea, your **EYE**. Make it about something greater than yourself to have a chance to grow.

The hardest part will be to find your first believer. But as soon as you are more than one heart beating at the same pace, the **synergy** will start to **attract** others looking for **Hope**. Soon enough a third person will join. Your *Momentum* has started to grow in both speed and power. From that point on, everything becomes easier.

"IT ONLY TAKES ONE TO START. TWO TO BELIEVE
AND THREE TO CONQUER."
DR BAK NGUYEN

It's been more than a month since I last wrote something worthy. The last time was in Toronto as I was wrapping up **Changing the world from a dental chair** in 5 days to defend my *Ernst & Young's nomination for entrepreneur of the year*. I made it! I got the book published within a month, got it released on Amazon and also got in studio to record the audiobook. What a crazy journey!

I then, went to speak at the Olympic Stadium as an anchor speaker, introducing my friend and banker Rouba Sakr who made the **Mdex & Co**'s project possible, went on to receive a promise of **$100 million** in investment, gain the heart of the crowd on the social media, especially on LinkedIn and at the **EY**'s evening for the *Entrepreneur of the year award...* to finally learn that I won't be made finalist this year... I knew that I had a thin financial past since I am at the head of three startups, but still, never before an entrepreneur went to such length to defend his nomination.

Was it hard on the ego? You have no idea. To face defeat publicly is hard, very hard on the ego. I didn't even have the excuse that I did not take it seriously since I went all in. But, as I said, it was not for me to decide who wins. But with all the amazing things happening, the creation of the *Board of Influence* and the other speaking events... I was simply too busy to crumble and have time for any self-pity.

I still have to face the crowd and tell them about my defeat. And I did, addressing them in a video, thanking **Ernst and Young** for the opportunity and the extra time to defend my nomination. Yes, you heard right, I am not giving up, I am still a nominee and will keep pushing the boundaries to make it into the next phase by 2019 or later on.

In the meantime, I will keep the momentum going in both my speaking engagements, my online videos and my books? At least two more are scheduled to be released this year, **Profession Health** and **Industries Disruptors**. I would have completed 7 books within 12 months. Not quite, there are still 29 days left for me to push it to 8 books within this year! Laugh as much as you want, but I was aiming for 12 on 12! Another *defeat!!!*

As my good friend and co-author, professor Robert Durand said:

But, I am Dr Bak, I do not fail, ever! Well, in fact, I failed often, I just do not give up and will be looking for ways to get back at those *minor road bumps.*

"MAKE LEVERAGE OF YOUR LIABILITIES
AND YOU WILL ALWAYS MOVE AHEAD!"

DR BAK NGUYEN

And I will live by my words. In the meantime, I have other fish to fry. Since I am saying **YES** to most proposals, I barely recognize my life anymore... It is surely exciting!

I still have to materialize that promise of **$100 Million**, on which I succeed to have a double down on since! Still another promise though, I am pretty close to announce the construction of another **Complex Mdex**. Yes, I will not wait around, I am still at the aim of the biggest turning tip of my industry with the **Mdex group** and more and more influential and powerful supports are joining in day after day!

By today, I can also disclose that I will be disrupting a new industry, the audiobooks world and will try to set **15 in 15**. Fifteen books in fifteen months. Eight more books to write within the next 3 months and 29 days. Will that be even possible?

The Power behind the Alpha, will be written with my best friend and wife, Tranie Vo. I dedicated a chapter in my first book, **Symphony of Skills** to my relationship with Tranie. I then, was invited to take the stand of an Entrepreneurial event for women. Women?! What do I know about women and entrepreneurship? It turned out that I had much to say and both, men and women were eager to hear more.

On stage, at my wife's birthday, I delivered a speech about how we made it as a team and how she was the real entrepreneur of the couple! She, *The Power behind the Alpha*, me the *mascot*! It was the best birthday gift ever, all the women in the room wanted to be her and to marry me... for about 30 minutes... I will be sharing the authoring of the book with Tranie, and, again, I will be listening, to not force her into my crazy *momentum* pace as I am writing to capture her purest essence and thoughts.

How do I get all of this done? By now, you all know that I will see them through. I am Dr Bak, I am a man of my word. It is all made possible through the **power of momentum**! To move from one area to the next, gaining speed and power and, replenishing on the way!

"ON THIN ICE, SPEED UP, THAT'S HOW
YOU WILL EVENTUALLY LEARN TO FLY!"
DR BAK NGUYEN

And here we are, at the introduction of my 8th book: **Momentum transfer**, a book co-written with my fitness coach and great friend: coach Dino Masson. Dino and I know each other pretty well and have collaborated throughout the years. I share a history of more than 5 years with Coach Dino Masson as we developed together the art of *Momentum transfer*. I have covered it in a chapter of my first book, **SYMPHONY OF SKILLS** to explain how I could write that fast, on top of my crazy schedule.

That was 11 months ago. Now, we are on a whole other level! It's not just about speed, but influence, creativity, depth, success, road bumps, comebacks and achieving the impossible, while gaining in speed and power! Coach Dino is a force of nature trapped in the mind of a teenager who is still about to discover his superpower! That's the friend. The coach, is an exceptional one, one dedicated to see others succeed, truly.

Coach Dino is more than a coach and even a friend, he was my confidant and the witness of my transformation from *Man* to *Alpha*, from *Entrepreneur* to *Disruptors*, from *Dreamer* to *Leader*.

That's the team, Coach Dino and Dr Bak co-writing this book, **MOMENTUM TRANSFER**, the secret to your superpower within! I have promised to say YES to everything or almost this year. I still have eight months to go until I can look back at my decision. So YES, I will be sharing with you my secret of **MOMENTUM** and will push the boundaries to the next level.

With Coach Dino helping me to analyze and channel my thought process so it becomes a recipe that you can all use in your everyday life, I have the hope that most of you, if not all of you, will feel included within those words. For your ambitions, your projects, to heal, to save the world, to find yourself, **MOMENTUM TRANSFER** is your way to find your inner power, to give meaning to both your words and your name!

> "THE DAY THAT ONE CONVINCED HIMSELF TO TAKE ACTION,
> THAT DAY, EVERYTHING STARTED TO SHIFT, FOR THE BETTER."
> DR BAK NGUYEN

I am glad to share with you, not just part of my journey but also my secrets. If anything, I feel empowered to share with you the knowledge of one of my greatest tools. The secret was crystal clear to me since I have mastered it on a daily basis, but to share the stage with my coach and friend Dino made the experience unique.

I was the one starting, he was the second one believing and as we shared, three, four, five and ten people started to gather around to listen and ask questions.

The very writing of this book is a *Momentum* and it is only starting to gain power and speed. Personally, this was my first finished book after nearly two months of interruption after the writing and publishing of **CHANGING THE WORLD FROM A DENTAL CHAIR**.

Even with all the attention and support, I was crushed when I finally received the letter, by the end of June, that letter wishing me luck but announcing that I won't be making it into the finalist phase.

That put a hole into my soul, my confidence. I kept my cool, but I had a hard time hiding my wounds. Two months went by until I finally found a way to *leverage my "failure"*. I needed to eclipse it with another win, a *Guinness World Record*. How about the most number of books written within 12 months! That was the spark to start my **EYE**.

I was in my 11th months since the beginning of my journey as an author. I still had one month left before my first anniversary as a writer. So I rebooted myself and got back in the game with hope. **MOMENTUM TRANSFER** is my coming back. To have the chance to share both the emotions and the excitement with Dino helped me to keep my motivation and focus on the prize.

I actually finished my part of this book within a little more than a week. Hours after the completion of this endeavour, I was already well immersed in my next book, **THE POWER BEHIND THE ALPHA**. The *Power of Momentum* allowed me to start the 12th month with 7 books and a chance to finish it with 9 books written.

To write two books on two completely different subjects within a month, back to back, was a first, even to me. But as I kept talking with Dino as he was writing his part of **MOMENTUM TRANSFER**, I was bathing in the essence and the *speed of Momentum*.

I have so much to do... but for reasons unclear to me, I still found pleasure and excitement to add more upon my shoulders. My three next instalments already had their subject and cover. Actually, the next seven are lining up at the starting line, waiting for the signal to explode into *Momentums* themselves.

My speed is found from within, as I believe that I serve a greater purpose than myself. The strength of my *Momentum* is founded as more and more people **share and believe in my story**, my journey.

"NOTHING FEELS MORE GRATEFUL THAN TO HAVE THE CHANCE TO TOUCH A LIFE FOR THE BETTER."

DR BAK NGUYEN

That's the feeling keeping me going and growing. My **EYE** is **stable** and **calm**. I found worth sharing my story to inspire others. I replenished myself by listening to the stories of the people I've touched.

As it is empowering,
I want more,
I do more,
I feel more!

I keep my heart open
And say **YES** as often as I can.
Actually, I say **YES** first
And then, I grow myself
Into fitting to what
I said **YES** to.

I cannot be any happier for coach Dino, which I mentored. He took actions and went to find his own **EYE**. I believe that his *Momentum* has now reached a stage of no return. In other words, he has launched. For years, he listened to my stories and shares my success as we were working out.

But, until lately, he was hearing as an external person, judging like a person in the public and riding as a spectator. The day that he convinced himself to take action, that day, everything started to shift for the better.

I remember that afternoon where he came to my house and said: "I am ready, ready to follow you." I was both happy and surprised. Happy because I knew that he will do great. Surprised since that took him a whole year before joining in something we shared for years together. He finally became a **believer**.

At first, he believes in me. Now that he found his **EYE**, he believes and bets on himself! This is not a race, it is a run to honour yourself, to find meaning to your life and to find worth in the service of others.

We all have unique powers to change the world and to make it into a better place, to us and to those who will be following after. Worth can only be found within the service of others. The more you serve, the more power and influence you'll have. Serving, power and influence, that's how to build *Momentum*, all taking root from your **EYE**.

With all the power and knowledge, the awareness that I am part of a bigger design helps me to keep perspective of the greater picture, helps me to stay humble.

That's the secret of **Momentum**. Have a taste of its power and you will never be the same again. May you find yours and start spreading Hope and light all around you.

Believe in yourself and embrace the possibilities of life. Life is greater than each of us. If you let it guide you, you'll be walking your destiny.

This is mine, may it inspires you to yours. This is the **POWER OF YES**, volume one. Welcome to the **Alphas**.

SOMEONE BETTER,
SOMEONE STRONGER,
SOMEONE HUNGRIER,
I BECAME MORE.
DR BAK NGUYEN.

SYNERGY IS THE CORE OF OUR POWER

-DR. BAK NGUYEN

CHAPTER 8

THE POWER BEHIND THE ALPHA

AUGUST 2018

BY DR BAK NGUYEN

I can spend all day writing about ambition, logic and leadership. I can talk to you for hours about philosophy, business and finance. But love... At the same time, it was my priority to write this book, **THE POWER BEHIND THE ALPHA**, to recognize the contribution of Tranie in our business success, her role in our love story, her presence in my life.

That's what I learned and discovered in life since my mind and heart got liberated from the burden of scars and the ladders of society. **I can have it all**, not all at the same time, but I can have everything I put my mind and heart into.

Actually, it is not completely true. I can have most of what I and Tranie put our minds into. Together, when we feel as one, there isn't much out of our reach. If I'm the mind, she's the heart; if I'm the Will, she's the means.

"SYNERGY IS THE CORE OF OUR POWER."

DR BAK NGUYEN

It's been about 24 hours since I finished my last chapter of **MOMENTUM TRANSFER**, my latest book with Coach Dino Masson. I wanted to finish the book in about a week, before my departure to Las Vegas for the delayed birthday trip of Tranie, my lovely wife and business partner.

Her birthday was a little more than a month ago, but since I couldn't book the plane tickets on time, we couldn't make it for her birthday. Since I ended up staying in Montreal that day, a friend invited me to speak at an event for businesswomen at the Saint-Joseph Basilica.

He gave me the confirmation that I would be speaking as one of the anchors of the event, not even 8 hours before the event!! My friend never does things halfway and he knows about my promise to say **YES** to everything for the next eight months...

So I accepted, obviously. I was initially planning to entertain Tranie for her birthday, to get her out for a fine dinner and shopping, trying to ease her deception about Vegas. Now, I had to announce to her that instead of the restaurant, we would be celebrating in a Basilica... She smiled gratefully and said that we still had 8 hours before the event anyway.

That's the woman Tranie is, always smiling and seeing life from the positive angle. So I was all hers for those first 8 hours of the day. An hour before the event, we were still shopping and having much fun! I remember how much we both laughed that day. Time was ticking and the event was approaching!

"I MUST HAVE BEEN EITHER CRAZY OR JUST VERY CONFIDENT."

DR BAK NGUYEN

I didn't prepare much before going on stage to open the Business Women's event. I am a man, what do I know about women's business and their challenges! That question, I had answered it once as I was writing my first book, **Symphony of Skills**, in which I dedicated a whole chapter to Tranie, talking about how she handled her role as a businesswoman always by my side. It turned out that I had much to say on the matter.

Thus, unprepared and a little cocky, I went on stage with a smile thinking that I would give Tranie the best birthday gift ever. I went on stage introducing myself and telling them how special that day was to me and to my wife; how I was grateful to Tranie for the kind of support and love she endorsed me with, each day, day after day, no matter the horizons; how she made me the man I am, standing confident and talking on stage to the world!

> "I AM THE MASCOT HERE! I AM JUST SURPRISED THAT IN MY COUPLE, WE CHOSE THE LEAST ATTRACTIVE TO BE SHOWCASED TO THE WORLD!"
> DR BAK NGUYEN

My speech was about business, the business that love made into a success. It was about the valse of two souls discovering the world together, one leading, the other empowering, until the next dance has the roles reversed, smoothly. That's the privilege and blessing that I am grateful for: to share Tranie's life and love. The crowd went insane! All the women, for about fifteen minutes, wanted to be Tranie and wanted, from the look in their eyes, to marry me... for fifteen minutes.

That night was a night that she will never forget. Tranie received my love and her birthday gift through the admiration and the envy of the crowd. After the conference, she was the one people were rushing to meet and shake hands with, more than me!!! I never saw Tranie as shy and as joyful at the same time!

I have to say that Tranie is a very reserved person. She does not crave for attention nor for opinions. She is just herself and lives her life with love and warmth. To make her the centre of attention of a crowd of businesswomen was the most original gift I could have thought of. It worked like a charm! That night, Tranie experienced a new, almost unknown feeling to her: **public recognition**.

By the next morning, I asked her how she felt. She loved the evening and the blush going through her cheeks as we were taking selfies with the women of the crowd, but she was grateful to have that private life she shared with me and our son William.

The feeling of public recognition was great but, like fine dining, only once in a while so it didn't lose its charm. It was her way to tell me that she still missed traveling... and that Vegas was still on her mind.

We made it happen, a month later. Here I am now, in Las Vegas, sitting in my room at the Venetian hotel, looking out the window as the sun rises, writing my next hymn of love to Tranie. How could I beat that evening at the Basilica, an evening that she will never forget?

By making something **legendary**! This time, it's not only a crowd of women in a Basilica that would be inspired by the love that Tranie clothed me with, it will be the whole world, women and men!

Writing **THE POWER BEHIND THE ALPHA** is my way to honour my wife and best friend. Nearly 20 years spent side by side, building a life, a family and a few businesses... About privacy? This is a book! If she does not wish it, she does not even have to go meet the crowd nor to take pictures... she can only be signing autographs...

"YOU CAN HAVE IT ALL, ONLY IF YOU ASK FOR IT
AND THAT YOU ARE READY TO RECEIVE IT!"
DR BAK NGUYEN

This whole book is about **love**.
Love is the starting point,
The excuse to meet,
The prelude to life.

Love is life,
Love is happiness,
Love is success.

This is my ode to love, my tribute to Tranie, my take to honour the women standing behind their men. Business is a man's world, but no man can stand without the support of a woman, a mother, a wife, a lover. Love who you want and be **grateful** for what you receive. That's how you can have a chance to find yourself, a *chance to happiness*.

"WE ARE BORN ALONE AND WE DIE ALONE."
A "GREAT MAN"

Both men and women proudly repeat those words as wisdom since. I apologize in advance, but what a **fat LIE**! If we cannot see the problem here, we are even more messed up than I thought! After being pushed out, after hours of labor, sometimes days, through the pain, the sweat, and the blood, as we were simply a passenger in our mother's body, we dare to say that we were born alone?!

"TO DIE ALONE MAY BE THE REFLECTION OF HOW YOU LIVED YOUR LIFE, BUT NO ONE IS EVER BORN ALONE."
DR BAK NGUYEN

That's the kind of injustice and the kind of insults we direct to those who love us the most. I am a man, born from a woman, raised by both parents and groomed into an **Alpha** from the love of a **power woman**. If anything, I cannot stay quiet in front of such ignorance or even worst, ungratefulness.

I have started by honoring my partner, Tranie. To give her a voice and a stand, in the hope of allowing more women to get inspired by her touch, her kindness, her wisdom. Tranie doesn't need the attention nor the love of the crowd. But she cares, she cares about those she loves. By writing this book, my hopes are that Tranie finds a new purpose and interest in her true worth, the love she can bring to the world.

Those were my words, fueling from Tranie's soul. You have no idea how much I poured my soul and heart into this endeavour. I had to empty myself completely to vibrate at Tranie's frequency and write from the answers she gave in her interviews. Doing so, I was so into it that I now feel what she feels. I went so deep that I got a hard time getting back into my own skin, my vibe after I was done with her chapters.

If anything, today, I am truly whole, with the ability to feel both elements, as different as they may be. Today, I have gained the inside knowledge of both the **Alpha** and the

Power. And once again, it was thanks to **love**, the love she inspired me, the love I owe her.

This book is a testimonial of love. It is not the universal recipe nor the blueprint for your own relationship. It's a guide to inspire you to find your own happiness, your own voice, to accept the love you have been given. Sometimes, love will come from far away, some times it's just in front of your eyes. Remember, if you don't have it yet, it's because you may not want it or you may not be ready yet! Shocking truth but still truth!

"THE ONLY WAY TO AVOID THE SHOCK IS TO BE GRATEFUL."

DR BAK NGUYEN

To be grateful for what you are.
To be grateful for who you were.
To be grateful for what's to come.
Gratitude is the only past
With a future.

Gratitude will lead you to love and **love** will lead you to **happiness**. Be ready to open your heart and to taste life in its abundance. It is your choice to make. It is your freedom to choose. We, Tranie and I, wish you luck and the happiest life.

Believe in yourself and embrace the possibilities of life. Life is greater than each of us. If you let it guide you, you'll be walking your destiny.

This is mine, may it inspires you to yours. This is the **POWER OF YES**, volume one. Welcome to the **Alphas**.

SOMEONE BETTER,
SOMEONE STRONGER,
SOMEONE HUNGRIER,
I BECAME MORE.
DR BAK NGUYEN.

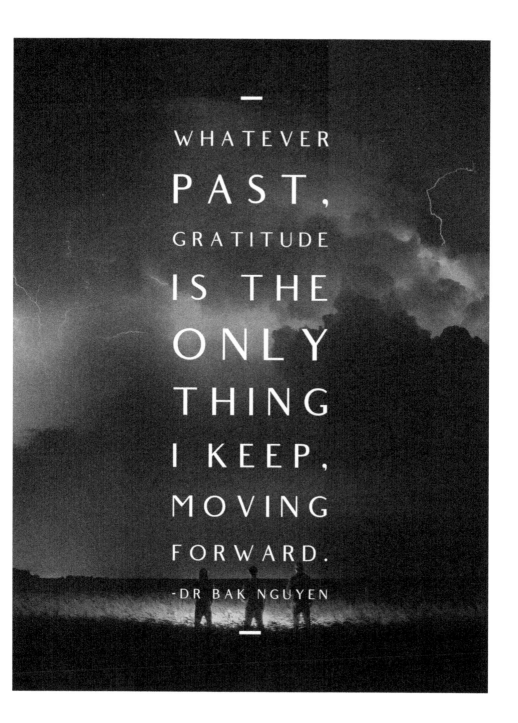

WHATEVER PAST, GRATITUDE IS THE ONLY THING I KEEP, MOVING FORWARD.

-DR BAK NGUYEN

CONCLUSION

BY DR BAK NGUYEN

This is 12 months writing. I may have failed to set the record of 12 books written over 12 months, but the record set of 9 books written over 12 months is a first worldwide! I believe that I set the bar high enough. Just kidding.

Now, it will be for me to beat my own score. As I mentioned earlier, I like the round numbers, the next round number is 15 books in 15 months. That one, I will hit!

If I started writing because I was terrified at the idea to speak after the former first lady of the USA, and that I kept writing because I kept waking up at 5 AM each morning, well, today, I am writing because it has become second nature and a cool personal challenge.

Yes I sleep 6-7 hours a day and still work and have leisure time. I even have the time to enjoy some TV shows on NETFLIX, sleeping shortly after it starts. If you are looking for a great way to sleep, the sound of the TV is one of my favorite.

The **POWER OF YES** was more than my journey writing, it was about me opening up and growing. Well, even if I officially started saying YES after Casey's speech, I realized that I started that journey 6 months earlier as I said YES to Thierry Lindor. I said YES to share my past and experience. That's how I started writing. Then, I kept writing. By the 4th book, I ran out of subjects about my past, so I opened up and started collaborating with co and guest authors.

If the 6th book, **INDUSTRIES DISRUPTORS**, was written in the present tense, from my 7th book, I needed to provoke things in my life to have something of worth to write about. That's my journey of **YES**.

And in the journey, you can feel its power. 12 months later, I am signing a milestone, both personal and on the world stage, writing 9 books within 12 months. Just like Casey, I am writing and moving on to the next, not looking back.

After 9 books, I now know how to write. By the next milestone, I will need to master the distribution channels, to have **Apple Books** and **Amazon** to publish and to push my titles. This will be for the next volume.

If you were looking for hope and a way to elevate yourself, you shared my story, step by step, as you walked in my footprints. I did and I moved on. Actually, the hardest to come back later on, as my co-authors deliver weeks after I have moved on to the next book.

"WRITING IS REALLY ABOUT FOCUS AND INTENSITY."
DR BAK NGUYEN

Those are the challenges I met, waiting for my co-authors and finding the time to come back to previous projects. I do that in between books, when I am not in a hurry writing 2 books a month. If the vibe was intense at the beginning of those projects, the drag took much of its charms away.

My biggest collaboration to this date was **PROFESSION HEALTH** with 2 co-authors and 5 guest authors. Then, **INDUSTRIES DISRUPTORS** who is still not completed, not my part, but my co-authors'. What keeps me opening up and welcome first-timers and strangers to join my vibe is that **POWER OF YES**.

Very little did I know that it will eventually empower me to welcome some of the people who changed my life, I name Sharon Lechter, co-author of **RICH DAD POOR DAD** a best-selling book, that sold more than 41 million copies worldwide! It's the **POWER OF YES** that made it happen. That and the law of **ATTRACTION**. Thank you Dr Letran for the introduction.

> **"WE ATTRACT WHAT WE GENUINELY ARE."**
> DR BAK NGUYEN

I also have my part of failure, writing with people who I parted ways from. Just like past team members, to them, I wish the best of luck and I move on, smiling at the good souvenirs and leaving all of it behind, good and bad. Fortunately, most never completed their chapters or never finalize our rights agreement, so I will eventually have to address those as I start cleaning my record.

I told you how hard for me it is to come back as I keep pushing forward faster and faster. Well, I will come back at those later on, eventually, in between my books and my challenges. I can't erase the past, no one can. Though, I have the power to edit it.

> ## "WHATEVER PAST, GRATITUDE IS THE ONLY THING I KEEP, MOVING FORWARD."
>
> DR BAK NGUYEN

So writing for the first 12 months, embracing life saying YES allowed me to reset myself after making sense of my past. It allowed me to be grateful and to understand where I came from, how and why I came to be. I had much fun looking back and revisiting. But now that it is done and catalogued in a narrative and a storyline, I can finally move forward free and lightweight.

Writing for 12 months and opening up rebooted my mind and freed my heart to embrace the NOW and its opportunities. I am still just starting my journey.

From now on, it is about NOW and the FUTURE. My past, I gracefully honor with **SYMPHONY OF SKILLS**, revisiting 20 years of entrepreneurship. My legacy and journey as a doctor, I made sense of it with **PROFESSION HEALTH**, with the desire to help my peers and colleague.

Little did I know that, 3 years later, I would be at the center of the heart of the reorganization of the healthcare industry at a global scale with my entrance in the world **TOP100 doctors** and being elected as a CHAIR of the **GLOBAL SUMMITS INSTITUTE**.

I gave 20 years of my life to the health industry. **INDUSTRIES DISRUPTORS** and **CHANGING THE WORLD FROM A DENTAL CHAIR** are my legacy and my promise to leverage upon my past to help my peers and friends.

And then, I started sharing, even more, I started sharing my current leverage and secret, opening up in **MOMENTUM TRANSFER**. Very little did I know that I will come to be known as a *Tornado*, worldwide, a kind and gentle *Alpha Force*. It all started with YES.

"GOOD THINGS HAPPEN WHEN YOU SAY YES."

DR BAK NGUYEN

And the bad? Well, saying YES will strengthen you, all of you. If what does not kills you make you stronger, YES will do that to your heart and soul.

Already, for the last 2 books, **MOMENTUM TRANSFER** and **THE POWER BEHIND THE ALPHA**, I came back on my footsteps, these two were chapters within book #1, **SYMPHONY OF**

SKILLS. I wrote these titles, not lacking inspiration, but realizing that I was just surfing an important subject.

Amongst these importances, honoring Tranie, my best friend, business partner and wife was a must. A must empowering womankind. Very gracefully, I lend her my words and my energy, writing her story and her perspective. Doing so, I grew even more, understanding the ripple effect and the collaterals.

Yes, after 12 months, I grew in confidence and my wording is more and more fluid, bolder and yet, more and more precise. If I flirted with power writing presidential speeches in **LEADERSHIP**, today, I do not need the label of **LEADERSHIP** to address the changes the world needs.

Today, I use everyday words and idea to touch and influence hearts and minds. Little did I know that it will take deep roots into my child's heart who will grow to become my must prolific co-author and biggest source of inspiration…

And what about the *Quest of Identity*, am I finally over that one? Writing **IDENTITY** was merely step one. The awakening that started a few years ago, from Dr Benkhalifa's teachings, found words and images as body in **IDENTITY**. Very little did I know that it will be the most important theme of my writing career.

Yes, by the time of this writing, I wrote 72 books, 2 years later, 3, since my first written words. Today, I am known as a *Tornado*, a *force of nature* and a *philosopher*, one with compassion and hope within his core. Those aren't my words, but those I repeat from the journey ahead of this first volume.

YES is a journey, at the end of each journey, a new one starts. Saying YES is to discover, life, powers and much fun. Embracing YES is embracing life, it is sometimes messy and it is alive. Writing about my journeys saying YES empowered my senses and instincts, leaving pride, doubt and fear behind. Yes, I grew. Yes, I became hungrier, faster, bigger. I opened my heart so much, that it is now inconceivable to close it down, even after my YESMAN challenge.

You picked this book up because you were curious. Maybe because you were looking for hope and for answers. This book is part of my story, part of my journey. It does not contain your answers but will give you the key to yours. If there is one thing I am doing is to grow your confidence and to empower you to listen to your heart. That's your *hope*.

I did so, sharing with you my past, medals and scars. I did so never pointing fingers but always taking the blame, even the 1% that was mine. And writing a day after the next, a week after the next, you feel the air picking up under your feet. You did fly with me for the last days, elevating your heart and spirit. You did so, riding my life.

Now if you feel ready, start surfing yours, your dreams, your past, your aspirations. Nothing is ever set in stone. As you do so, you can always come back for another ride with me. **THE POWER OF YES**, volume two and three are right around the corner.

"TO GROW, ONE MUST OPEN UP. IT IS IMPOSSIBLE TO OPEN UP AND NOT TO FEEL. FEEL TO GROW."

DR BAK NGUYEN

Revisiting my books and chapters, I almost forgot that I use to write poems and songs. Maybe those will come back after the completion of this book. Sing and stop being an animal, one afraid and lost, one insecure, and who bow to shadow, fear and doubt.

My quest of freedom brought me to yield and master many powers, most of them more powerful than the conventional meaning of the concept we came to accept.

"A FREE HEART IS THE MOST POWERFUL HEART."

DR BAK NGUYEN

And it will beat stronger, deeper and last much longer. Believe in yourself and embrace the possibilities of life. Life is greater than each of us. If you let it guide you, you'll be walking your destiny.

This is mine, may it inspires you to yours. This is the **POWER OF YES**, volume one. Welcome to the **Alphas**.

SOMEONE BETTER,
SOMEONE STRONGER,
SOMEONE HUNGRIER,
I BECAME MORE.
DR BAK NGUYEN.

From Canada, **Dr BAK NGUYEN**, Nominee Ernst and Young Entrepreneur of the year, Grand Homage Lys DIVERSITY, and LinkedIn & TownHall Achiever of the year. Dr Bak is a cosmetic dentist, CEO and founder of Mdex & Co. His company is revolutionizing the dental field. Speaker and motivator, he wrote 72 books over 36 months accumulating many world records (to be officialized).

- **ENTREPRENEURSHIP**
- **LEADERSHIP**
- **QUEST OF IDENTITY**
- **DENTISTRY AND MEDICINE**
- **PARENTING**
- **CHILDREN BOOKS**
- **PHILOSOPHY**

In 2003, he founded Mdex, a dental company upon which in 2018, he launched the most ambitious private endeavour to reform the dental industry, Canada wide. Philosopher, he has close to his heart the quest of happiness of the people surrounding him, patients and colleagues alike. In 2020, he launched an International collaborative initiative named **THE ALPHAS** to share knowledge and to Entrepreneurs and Doctors to thrive through the Greatest Pandemic and Economic depression of our time.

In 2016, he co-found with Tranie Vo, Emotive World Inc, a tech research company to use technology to empower happiness and sharing. U.A.X. the ultimate audio experience is the landmark project on which the team is advancing, utilizing the technics of the movie industry and the advancement in ARTIFICIAL INTELLIGENCE to save the book industry and to upgrade the continuous education space.

These projects have allowed Dr Nguyen to attract interests from the international and diplomatic community and he is now the center of a global discussion in the wellbeing and the future of the health profession. It is in that matter that he shares his thoughts and encourages the health community to share their own stories.

"It's not worth it go through it alone! Together, we stand, alone, we fall."

Motivational speaker and serial entrepreneur, philosopher and author, from his own words, Dr Nguyen describes himself as a dentist by circumstances, an entrepreneur by nature and a communicator by passion.He also holds recognitions from the Canadian Parliament and the Canadian Senate.

www.DrBakNguyen.com

AMAZON - APPLE BOOKS - KINDLE - SPOTIFY - APPLE MUSIC

ULTIMATE AUDIO EXPERIENCE

A new way to learn and enjoy Audiobooks. Made to be entertaining while keeping the self-educational value of a book, UAX will appeal to both auditive and visual people. UAX is the blockbuster of the Audiobooks.

UAX will cover most of Dr Bak's books, and is now negotiating to bring more authors and more titles to the UAX concept. Now streaming on Spotify, Apple Music and available for download on all major music platforms. Give it a try today!

www.DrBakNguyen.com

AMAZON - APPLE BOOKS - KINDLE - SPOTIFY - APPLE MUSIC

FROM THE SAME AUTHOR
Dr Bak Nguyen

www.DrBakNguyen.com

THE POWER OF YES 5 074
VOLUME FIVE: ALPHA
BY Dr BAK NGUYEN

THE POWER OF YES 6 075
VOLUME SIX: PERSPECTIVE
BY Dr BAK NGUYEN

.

www.DrBakNguyen.com

AMAZON - APPLE BOOKS - KINDLE - SPOTIFY - APPLE MUSIC

DR.

Bak Nguyen

Printed in Great Britain
by Amazon